The Glory and the Burden

THE GLORY
– *and* –
THE BURDEN

*The American Presidency
from FDR to Trump*

ROBERT SCHMUHL

University of Notre Dame Press
Notre Dame, Indiana

University of Notre Dame Press
Notre Dame, Indiana 46556
undpress.nd.edu

All Rights Reserved

Copyright © 2019 by University of Notre Dame

Published in the United States of America

Library of Congress Control Number: 2019021436

ISBN: 978-0-268-10673-7 (hardback)

ISBN: 978-0-268-10675-1 (WebPDF)

ISBN: 978-0-268-10676-8 (Epub)

∞ *This book is printed on acid-free paper.*

For

WILLIAM HUDSON GILES

*Who, in the twilight of his great
collegiate career, kindly guided
a wayward student with wisdom,
humor, and friendship that endure*

—— CONTENTS ——

—— PROLOGUE ——

My fascination with presidents and the American presidency began innocently enough when I was a small child, through the kindness of a hotel bellhop. On a family vacation to Kansas City, we were staying at the Hotel Muehlebach, and my grandmother happened to be a Muehlebach and one of the hotel's founders. Ralph, the bellhop, indulged a befreckled squirt's obsession with collecting autographs of big-league baseball players—most teams stayed at the Muehlebach when they played in Kansas City from the mid-1950s into the 1960s. But one time, no doubt in an attempt to broaden a youth's limited horizons, he proposed a new adventure. Instead of pointing out players in the lobby, whom I could corner into signing the baseball I unfailingly carried around, Ralph recommended a tour of one of the hotel's restricted areas: the presidential suite. As we went up on the elevator, he patiently listed the numerous presidents who had stayed there, devoting most of his monologue to Harry Truman.

Beginning with his boyhood in Independence, and during his later years in Kansas City, Truman maintained strong connections to his stomping ground of western Missouri. Indeed, as I subsequently learned, the Muehlebach became known as

"White House West" during his nearly eight years in office. What does an eager, young visitor do amid such historic surroundings? While Ralph was turning on lights around the penthouse, I decided to sit at the piano Truman used to play and plunked on the keys with wild abandon. Ralph kept this inharmonious interlude to himself, and, for once, I didn't get into trouble.

Learning about Truman—we also visited the Truman Library and Museum in Independence—served as just the beginning. By the earliest years of high school, I knew I wanted to work in journalism, so keeping up with the news (including coverage of Washington) became a daily and rewarding commitment. Being called "prematurely old" by classmates and others should have hurt my adolescent feelings, but it really didn't.

During senior year of high school, besides spending many more hours at the local newspaper as a part-time reporter than I did bookworming to prepare for college, I wrote a major research paper, the subject of which turned out to be "Barry Goldwater and Conservatism." Why a seventeen-year-old decided to devote forty pages of juvenile scholarship to a losing presidential candidate and his cause two years after his landslide loss in 1964, I can't remember. Yet heeding the teacher's advice, I sent a copy of what I had written to the man who had run and led the movement. In his response, Goldwater said he "enjoyed reading" my immature effort at erudition, adding a concluding sentence: "I appreciate this more than words can ever express and I wish you success and happiness as you enter college." (There was a nice compliment for my treatment of conservatism, but he didn't address one of the paper's conclusions: "It is unlikely that a conservative will run again for the presidency in the next few elections." Ronald Reagan wouldn't win his first term as California's governor until November 1966, and he was, as it turned out, four campaign cycles away from winning the White House in 1980.)

During my undergraduate years—the late 1960s and into the spring of 1970—it was impossible to avoid keeping a close eye on the serving presidents. Lyndon Johnson and Richard Nixon—with their controversial decision making about the Vietnam War—concentrated the mind of every male facing the possibility of being drafted. Though I composed numerous dispatches for newspapers and magazines about this tumultuous era, it wasn't until graduate school and the Watergate investigation that I definitely decided that contemporary political affairs, particularly the presidency, would be the focus of my teaching and writing. Until then, I'd followed a traditional, rather unexciting path in pursuit of a doctorate specializing in American literature and American studies while writing fugitive pieces of journalism to stay in training. What could be more conventional or predictable for a graduate student interested in both literary and journalistic matters than a dissertation about Mark Twain's autobiographical narratives?

However, during a writing course I was teaching as a graduate instructor in 1973, a student raised her hand and wanted to know why so many people on television and elsewhere were talking about what was then referred to as "the Watergate affair." She inquired with innocent sincerity, "What really happened?" It was a question and a class session I'll never forget. For the remainder of the period, as I explained the break-in at the Democratic Party headquarters at the Watergate complex and other nefarious deeds that ultimately resulted in Nixon's resignation a year later, everyone in the classroom seemed uncharacteristically alert and genuinely curious. Somehow or other, worrying about split infinitives or the proper placement of adverbs faded in importance.

During this time, I happened to be reading *The Education of Henry Adams*. One sentence in the book kept returning to my thinking: "The progress of evolution from President Washington to President Grant, was alone evidence to upset Darwin." I wondered what Adams might have said about Nixon, and it's a question I've asked myself about subsequent presidents since then.

While serving my last years in graduate school, I was lucky enough to jump from the English Department to a new center that had been established in the wake of Watergate and was dedicated to the study of American institutions, including the presidency, Congress, and journalism. There I was able to teach and to do research. Good fortune continued when a regular faculty position in American studies at another university followed this five-year immersion in contemporary affairs.

Before too long, besides teaching an assortment of classes, I was writing journal articles, op-ed columns, and lengthy magazine essays about political topics, from time to time over the next few decades publishing collections of previously published articles or books that amplified my shorter works. Beginning in the 1980s, each presidential campaign became something of a marathon talkathon for providing commentary and punditry of one kind or another. Print reporters would call for a paragraph or two of analysis, and radio or television producers would request sound bites or longer interviews. In due course, invitations arrived asking me to lecture on the current White House occupants or the presidency in front of audiences, both domestic and foreign.

Journalistic shorthand has occasionally branded me a "political scientist," which I most assuredly am not. Other pithy phrases have described me as a "politics professor" or, somewhat more intriguingly, a "political professor." The late, incomparable Christopher Hitchens went so far in an essay for *Harper's Magazine* to say I was an academic "who specializes in the country's peculiar fascination with personality politics." More generalist than specialist, I try to keep vigilant watch on the Oval Office and the institution of the presidency. Is a developing trend worth pointing out and analyzing? Are changes involving the institution affecting the conduct of its occupants? Have American politics since the 1960s made day-to-day governing more difficult?

For instance, back in 2011, I wrote a column for the *Chicago Tribune* pointing out that, if Barack Obama won reelection in 2012, the United States would have three consecutive two-term presidents, a situation that had occurred only one other time in history and under vastly different circumstances—with the presidencies of Thomas Jefferson, James Madison, and James Monroe between 1801 and 1825. What could that possibly mean? Why? Was the tendency for retention strong enough among voters that there might be four in a row after the election of 2020?

No person is objective. All of us harbor biases and prejudices to one degree or another. In teaching, writing, and speaking, I work to focus on interpretable facts and their contexts, specifically words and actions, with as much impartiality as one can muster. To the often-asked question about my favorite president, I respond with one last name but two figures: Theodore Roosevelt, a Republican, and his fifth cousin Franklin, a Democrat.

When requested to pass judgment on the most consequential president since World War II, I usually say that John Kennedy, a Democrat, possessed an abundance of promise but didn't have the chance to complete his service, while Ronald Reagan, a Republican, served eight full years (something his five immediate predecessors couldn't accomplish), restored a spirit of faith in the nation, and retired with historians composing studies about the significance of "the Age of Reagan." If prompted for a more robust explanation, I say the Gipper's popularity certainly helped his vice president, George H. W. Bush, win an electoral victory in 1988, a first for a sitting number 2 since Martin Van Buren, Andrew Jackson's understudy, in 1836. Reagan also announced he had been diagnosed with Alzheimer's disease the weekend before the midterm election of 1994, which turned out to be a Republican landslide. (The GOP took control of the House of Representatives by gaining fifty-four seats and of the Senate by capturing eight.) Commentators dubbed what happened "the Republican Revolution." I argued in a commentary for the *Christian Science Monitor* that all the attention to Reagan's revelation of his illness right before balloting might have been an unmeasured yet influential factor in the outcome, an explanation a political scientist would never hazard. My analysis was based in part on an uncomplicated observation: timing is everything—in both acting and politics.

After nearly fifty years in classrooms across four continents—and being no longer "prematurely old" but certifiably senior—it seemed time to set down some summary reflections on presidential subjects, and the arrival of Donald J. Trump on the political—and world—stage became the appropriate provocation. His election as president in 2016 represented more than the ascent to America's highest elective office of someone without a day's experience in either government or the military. The victory by the business mogul and media celebrity reflected just how much today's presidency and US politics differ from those of not so long ago. The word *unprecedented* kept appearing in reportage about Trump. How he won—rallies rather than advertising, imprecise statements instead of specific proposals, strict privacy related to his taxes in lieu of the usual disclosure, and all the rest—proved that time-honored political practices could be challenged and often broken. Though Trump's triumph was unpredicted by prognosticators and bookies, it was not totally unpredictable when you examine larger patterns and trends in the presidency and in American politics during recent decades.

Self-branded as a modern-day Midas with unrivaled celebrity appeal, Trump's public persona—complete with its massive magnification by the media—tends to overshadow and obscure the political forces that helped propel him to the White House. To be sure, he portrays himself as a Washington outsider—but so has every winning presidential candidate (except George H.W. Bush) since Jimmy Carter in 1976. How about the emphasis on personality instead of party credentials? Carter's toothy smile and pledge never to lie signaled that the dominance of establishment, insider politics was in decline—and citizens' say, via primaries and caucuses, could be decisive.

Ironically, as the parties have become weaker institutionally, we have seen partisanship increase to the point of polarization or even tribalism as defining traits of Washington's political conduct. Concepts of compromise and consensus seem quaintly anachronistic in an environment that favors winning, whatever the cost, and vanquishing one's opponent in the process. Transacting the federal government's business without cross-party support—just as not a single Republican in the House of Representatives or Senate voted in favor of The Patient Protection and Affordable Care Act in 2010, no Democrat said "yea" to the Tax Cuts and Jobs Act of 2017—is increasingly de rigueur. And, to be more precise, controversial legislation is becoming more transparently partisan when the legislative and executive branches are controlled by the same party.

Trump, viewed in the round and beyond himself, is the embodiment of several existing forces that wittingly or unwittingly he effectively exploited and, in some instances, pushed to extremes. He's a distinctive, often indescribable effect of this particular political and cultural time, who is also causing our democracy to change more and more in ways that reflect his image. How long his brand of politics—defiance of institutional norms as though they never existed, constant direct communication with his base of support, unfiltered criticism of government agencies, confrontational attacks aimed at any perceived opponent, and all the rest—will be influential is a mystery of the Trump drama and is territory for someone else to explore. Here we are interested primarily in assessing what's already happened, with the patterns and trends of the recent past providing the backbone of this book.

Those patterns and trends, along with their effects on the people who occupy the Oval Office, deserve careful delineation. Before Trump, the last New Yorker to call 1600 Pennsylvania Avenue home was Franklin D. Roosevelt. Revolutionary changes have occurred in the presidency from FDR's era to Trump's time, and the circumstances that gave rise to those changes deserve explication and evaluation. As I'll explain, the office is shaped by the occupant, while the occupant is shaped by external forces (increasingly these are cultural ones related to communication) that produce the environment for campaigning and then for governing. Those realities are related but different.

Recent changes, however, coexist with historic continuities and institutional complexities. In 1797, while serving as vice president, Thomas Jefferson admitted in a letter to Eldridge Gerry that "the second office of this government is honorable & easy, the first is but a splendid misery." Using an oxymoron (such as "splendid misery") to describe the presidency became something of a lexical tradition. Less than a year after moving into the White House, Andrew Jackson noted in a letter to Robert J. Chester, "I can with truth say mine is a situation of dignified slavery." Four years before his election in 1856, James Buchanan wrote to his friend Nahum Capen, "The Presidency is a distinction far more glorious than the crown of any hereditary monarch in Christendom; but yet it is a crown of thorns." More recently, service in the nation's highest office has been characterized as a "glorious burden," a two-word quotation appropriated from a poem by Goethe. Since 2000, the Smithsonian's National Museum of American History in Washington, DC, has featured a permanent exhibition called "The American Presidency: A Glorious Burden." (Interestingly, for trivia aficionados, that phrase, in another manifestation, word order, and context, became the title of a book—*The Burden and the Glory* (1964)—that collected Kennedy's last speeches and statements from the twenty-three months before his assassination on November 22, 1963.)

For years, the following sign greeted anyone visiting or just passing by the edifice-cum-monument at 1600 Pennsylvania Avenue: "Since 1792, the White House has become symbolic of the American presidency throughout the world. While the Capitol represents the freedom and ideals of the Nation, the White House stands for the power and statesmanship of the chief executive." Called the "President's Palace," the "Presidential Mansion," or the "Executive Mansion" before 1901, "White House—Washington" was the name Theodore Roosevelt put on his stationery. The label took hold and stuck. "Palace?" "Mansion?" No. But "House"—without alluding to the principal resident and closer to the nickname you hear frequently now: "The People's House."

Look around from the street and a certain majestic glory is in full view. Should you see the president leave the White House as you are rubbernecking, the motorcade roaring by seems endless, each vehicle carrying staff with specific responsibilities; or you might observe the helicopter Marine One departing to take the president on the five-minute flight to Joint Base Andrews, in Maryland, to board the imposingly impressive Air Force One. In either case, grandeur meets power, and your head shakes. Yet if you take in the whole scene of what the welcoming sign calls "the most famous address in the United States," the house also resembles a modern-day fortress—with high fences, multiple concrete barriers, well-armed guards, bomb-sniffing dogs, weaponry on the roof, and all the rest. Along with the glory, the burden of constant security stalks a president's every step—and daily deliberations. The glory and the burden, both magnified to degrees approaching the unimaginable, come with the job from inauguration through the final hour of service.

One can hope that more attention to the vagaries and vicissitudes related to the wielding of (in the Constitution's phrase) "executive Power"—with a capital *P*—will help citizens better understand not only the office, with its duties and responsibilities, but also their own civic role as they consider what incumbents are doing and where candidates seeking the presidency want to take the country.

Americans tend to think about the White House in individualistic terms—a succession (to this point) of men, making decisions and offering leadership on domestic and international affairs. This personalization of the presidency is inevitable but also limiting. The institution—its definition, its development, its opportunities, its boundaries, and its other dimensions—often shapes the conduct of America's head of state, highest governmental executive, commander in chief, principal policy initiator, top diplomat, and party leader. This book attempts to take a broader view at the presidency in its contemporary context. Why is the office as it is today, and can we expect tomorrow to be markedly different?

Along the way, we shall also discuss the current (and, in the view of many, dubious) state of American politics. Back in 1979, political scientist Theodore J. Lowi noted in the preface to the second edition of his influential study *The End of Liberalism: The Second Republic of the United States* that "this book is dedicated to the proposition that the most fundamental political problem of our time *is* our politics" (xiii). One could argue that the problem he identified four decades ago has not improved but become much worse—reaching, in the opinion of many thoughtful observers, a breaking point. What will it take to make American politics work more effectively for the public at large in the years to come?

At a time when the United States looks more divided than united, with the political conduct in Washington a daily (and often depressing) reminder of our contemporary disunion, this series of essays seeks to explain how we arrived at this civic crossroads. An informed, inquiring citizenry serves as the foundation of a well-functioning, participatory democratic republic. Each of us has a considerable stake in the success or failure of the one person who has the authority and responsibility for representing all the American people and the country's interests at home and around the world.

— ONE —

Consequences of Change

During the first third of the twentieth century, six candidates of the Republican Party won the White House. Woodrow Wilson, who served as president between 1913 and 1921, was the only Democrat to interrupt the GOP sequence of William McKinley, Theodore Roosevelt, William Howard Taft, Warren Harding, Calvin Coolidge, and Herbert Hoover. Underscoring the party's dominance back then, each victorious Republican received over 50 percent of the popular vote in 1900, 1904, 1908, 1920, 1924, and 1928. By contrast, Wilson failed to receive a majority in either the 1912 or 1916 election.

For the next thirty-six years, from 1933 until 1969, four Democrats—Franklin D. Roosevelt, Harry Truman, John Kennedy, and Lyndon Johnson—occupied the Oval Office, and there was just one Republican: Dwight Eisenhower. Like Wilson, Eisenhower broke one-party control of the executive branch for

1

an eight-year period (1953–61). Unlike Wilson, Eisenhower garnered impressive popular vote majorities twice—54.9 percent in 1952 and 57.4 in 1956.

Eisenhower's first election flipped the White House from the Democrats to the Republicans, but Kennedy returned it to the Democratic side eight years later. From then on, the presidential pendulum has continued to swing regularly back and forth between the two parties: to the Republicans with the 1968 election of Richard Nixon; to the Democrats in 1976, when Jimmy Carter prevailed; to Ronald Reagan and the GOP in 1980; to the Democrats and Bill Clinton in 1992; to the Republicans and George W. Bush in 2000; to Barack Obama and the Democratic Party in 2008; and back to the Republican side in 2016, with Donald Trump as the party's standard-bearer. Since the election of 1952, there have been *nine* party changes in the presidency, a considerably greater frequency than the electoral shifts that took place for nearly seven decades during the previous century, which featured fifty-two years of Republican presidents and forty-eight years of Democrats. A newfound volatility has replaced relative stability in the nation's highest office. Except for the twelve-year stretch (1981–93) covering the presidencies of Reagan and the senior George Bush, the White House has bounced from one major party to the other every eight years since the seven post–World War II elections: in 1960, 1968, 1976, 1992, 2000, 2008, and 2016. In 1980, the change occurred more quickly, after just a single term.

What's behind this form of partisan change after such pronounced continuity, including twenty consecutive years of Democratic administrations from 1933 to 1953? Have Americans become politically jumpy, prone to electoral anxiety that results in the favoring of one party over the other with noteworthy regularity? Are some voters, conditioned by the media to change channels or websites on impulse, more inclined of late to switch allegiances out of civic boredom or frustration? Are there other causes?

Viewed in context, constitutional, procedural, and cultural reasons have played significant roles in shaping the environment for electing a president that's developed since the middle of the twentieth century. They intersect with each other and have produced a very different political and electoral landscape from the previous five decades. That new landscape, in turn, has resulted in the election to the White House of different kinds of people, each of whom has become the world's most powerful person.

Let's be specific. The Twenty-Second Amendment establishing a two-term limit for a White House occupant was proposed by Congress on March 21, 1947, and formally ratified by the requisite number of states on February 27, 1951. Interpreted by many observers as revenge by Republican majorities in the House of Representatives and the Senate, rather than reform, the amendment was in part intended to prevent a popular political figure, such as Franklin Roosevelt, from winning more than two presidential elections. (During the six decades from 1931 to 1995, the GOP controlled both chambers of Congress for only four years: 1947–49 and 1953–55.)

The amendment serves as a formal, mandated check on the chief official of the executive branch. It also dictates that after two winning White House campaigns, the victor must by law retreat to the political sidelines. A definite, legally fixed end date means, among other things, that a president becomes, in effect, a lame duck in chief during a second term. Until the limit came into effect, the country's foremost political leader could exert influence with more robust force and meaning. The door remained ajar, at least potentially, to future dealings between the White House and Capitol Hill. As it is now, members of the House and Senate are looking ahead to their own elections— and self-preservation—and a president often has to rely more on personal persuasion than institutional clout to accomplish the goals on the administration's to-do list. To a certain extent, the balance of power shifts in the second term, with Congress the principal beneficiary.

James MacGregor Burns and Susan Dunn cogently summarized the situation in a 2006 *New York Times* commentary when they wrote, "A second-term president will, in effect, automatically be fired within four years. Inevitably his influence over

Congress, and even his authority over the sprawling executive branch, weaken. His party leadership frays as presidential hopefuls carve out their own constituencies for the next election. Whether the president is trying to tamp down scandal or push legislation, he loses his ability to set the agenda." They go on to observe that a second termer also loses "accountability to the people," which is "at the heart of a democratic system." In everyday life, if we know someone will be leaving a position at a particular time, our internal calculus for dealing with the person changes from what we would do if we had no knowledge of an exact departure date. That's human nature. And that person's proposal for a new initiative might get buried or a decision related to an action could be delayed until the clock runs out and there might be a different dynamic to consider.

The public's attitude toward a political figure who is mandated to leave office is that change is definitely on the horizon. Granted, the two-term tradition began with George Washington, but tradition is vastly different from a constitutional amendment. Before Franklin Roosevelt won four successive campaigns—1932, 1936, 1940, and 1944—Ulysses S. Grant in the nineteenth century and Wilson in the early twentieth tried to convince their parties (Grant as a Republican and Wilson as a Democrat) that they deserved a third term. As it happened, neither succeeded, and debate about presidents serving more than eight years in office roiled the 1940 race. Popular campaign buttons that year read, "I'm against the 3rd term: Washington Wouldn't, Grant Couldn't, Roosevelt Shouldn't," "Out! Stealing Third!" and "No Third Term-ites!"

Still, the barrier even to contemplate an administration's lasting longer than eight years is a factor in the minds of voters as they evaluate presidential candidates. There have been efforts (by both Democrats and Republicans) to repeal the amendment, but they haven't received broad support. Should they? Would more time for executive leadership result in sustained continuity of governance or concentrate power in the hands of one person in ways that jeopardize the democratic equilibrium? (Chapter 5 pursues these questions in detail.)

Besides the constitutional check to term limits—check 22, if you will—seeking the presidency has radically changed in recent decades. Even the timing for becoming a White House candidate has become more of a personal decision in recent years. Politically ambitious men and women more frequently look in the mirror and begin humming "Hail to the Chief." In *President Kennedy: Profile of Power*, Richard Reeves dates the new thinking for deciding whether to pursue the highest office to Kennedy's run in 1960:

Looking back, it seemed to me that the most important thing about Kennedy was not a great political decision, though he made some, but his own political ambition. He did not wait his turn. He directly challenged the institution he wanted to control, the political system. After him, no one else wanted to wait either, and few institutions were rigid enough or flexible enough to survive impatient ambition—driven challenges. He believed (and proved) that the only qualification for the most powerful job in the world was wanting it. His power did not come from the top down nor from the bottom up. It was an ax driven by his own ambition into the middle of the system, biting to the center he wanted for himself. (14)

Since Kennedy's time, what's striking is how many first-time presidential aspirants have run and triumphed: Carter in 1976, Clinton in 1992, George W. Bush in 2000, Obama in 2008, and Trump in 2016. Reagan, always folksy and good-natured, even challenged an incumbent (Ford) in his own Republican Party in 1976, before winning in 1980. Running at age sixty-nine, he knew he didn't want to wait any longer.

In addition to the transformation in personal decision making, institutional changes have been critically important in the selection of presidential candidates during the most recent decades. Most significantly, the Democratic Party's national convention in 1968 was responsible for initiating the reconsideration and reform of nominating procedures. In many ways, the office itself and the type of occupants it attracts changed as a result of the new rules for selecting nominees that, over time, both major parties adopted. The Democratic National Convention in Chicago in August 1968 followed this sequence of dramatic events: Senator Eugene McCarthy's challenge to Lyndon Johnson's possible candidacy, President Johnson's decision not to seek reelection, Senator Robert Kennedy's assassination as he campaigned for the nomination, not to mention the fatal shooting of the Reverend Martin Luther King Jr. and its violent aftershocks. However, Johnson's vice president, Hubert H. Humphrey, who had not formally entered a single primary that year, still secured the presidential nomination. McCarthy's supporters and opponents of the Vietnam War argued at the convention—marked by bloody clashes between the Chicago police and demonstrators—that the Democrats weren't exactly democratic in choosing the party's standard-bearer, who was, in effect, LBJ's understudy and a key member of an often-reviled administration.

The consequence of the full-throated criticism directed at a closed process was the creation of the Commission on Party Structure and Delegate Selection in early 1969. In its meetings and documents, the commission stressed the importance of opening up the election or choice of nominating delegates to more people in transparent ways that advanced self-governance. Citizen involvement, particularly through participation in primaries and caucuses (in this new nominating process) would replace backroom bargaining by political insiders in what were, at the time, referred to as smoke-filled rooms, stereotypically populated by cigar-chomping male officeholders and operators. An immediate effect of the commission was a proliferation of Democratic nominating contests—the number of primaries almost doubled, from fifteen in 1968 to twenty-eight in 1972. (George McGovern served as chair of the commission until 1971, when he decided to run for the Democratic presidential nomination. Navigating the new system he helped to design, the South Dakota senator did indeed become the party's nominee, but he lost decisively to the incumbent, Richard Nixon, earning just 37.5 percent of the popular vote, compared with Nixon's 60.7 percent. McGovern carried just one state, Massachusetts, and the District of Columbia.)

Included in the commission's guidelines is the following paragraph: "The 1968 Convention indicated no preference between primary, convention, and committee systems for choosing delegates. The Commission believes, however, that committee systems by virtue of their indirect relationship to the delegate selection process, offer fewer guarantees for a full and meaningful opportunity to participate than the other systems." Though the Republicans were somewhat slower in expanding the nominating process beyond party officials, the emphasis on openness and citizen selection took hold nationally. In short, presidential politics radically changed, and the consequences couldn't be predicted.

A critical year in this evolving process was 1976. Republicans had primary contests in twenty-eight states that year, with President Gerald Ford battling Reagan, a former two-term California governor, all the way to the party's convention in Kansas City. Ford ultimately received the nomination with 1,187 delegates to Reagan's 1,070. On the Democratic side, Jimmy Carter, a one-term Georgia governor, took on some sixteen other hopefuls, of varying degrees of seriousness, and Democrats conducted twenty-eight primaries, the same number as the Republicans. Carter dominated the delegate competition, and political analysts that year noted that "a candidate-centered" process had officially replaced "a party-centered" one, with the Georgian's success described by one observer as the end point of "the old boss-dominated system."

Early in the 1976 campaign, newspaper headlines asked a two-word question: "Jimmy Who?" But Carter's triumph over Ford in the November general election began a significant trend in presidential history. The six presidents who preceded Carter were either Washington insiders (Harry Truman, John Kennedy, Lyndon Johnson, Richard Nixon, Gerald Ford) or known as well connected in the nation's capital (Dwight Eisenhower). Carter was a bona fide outsider, with no experience in federal office and a total of eight years in state government (four as a state senator and four as governor). Presidents who followed Carter included these other Washington outsiders: Ronald Reagan, Bill Clinton, George W. Bush, Barack Obama, and Donald Trump. George H. W. Bush with eight years as vice president and extensive service in appointed positions (CIA director, United Nations ambassador, etc.) certainly qualified as an insider; however, his election in 1988 was, in part, a referendum on Reagan's record and was interpreted by some pundits as "the Gipper's third term." To be sure, Obama was a US senator when he sought the White House in 2008. But he had completed less than four years of a six-year term, and much of his time in the Senate was actually devoted to pursuing the Democratic presidential nomination. He arrived in Washington in early 2005 after almost eight years as a state senator in Illinois.

Trump's unexpected victory in 2016 was the apogee of outsider achievement on the presidential level. A candidate with no political, governmental, or military experience took on sixteen contenders, many of whom were governors and senators, in the Republican nominating contests. And the business tycoon/media celebrity prevailed in the fall against Hillary Clinton—a former First Lady, who was also a former US senator, as well as a former secretary of state. Strikingly, though, she was by no means the first well-known insider to lose a White House race in our new political environment, with its more explicit emphasis on openness and civic engagement from the nominating period through to Election Day. Other identifiable insiders who have lost presidential elections since party elders abandoned their smoky spaces include Walter Mondale in 1984, the senior George Bush in 1992, Bob Dole in 1996, Al Gore in 2000, John Kerry in 2004, and John McCain in 2008. In each case, Washington expertise proved less important in most voters' minds than the desire to place someone not associated with Washington at the head of the federal government.

What's behind this dramatic shift from supporting, say, a senator like Kennedy, or three former vice presidents like Truman, Johnson, and Nixon, who had also been senators? According to survey research in public opinion, one of the first measurements of "trust" in federal government took place in 1958. Almost three-quarters of those surveyed (73 percent) responded that they trusted "the government in Washington always or most of the time." The number rose to 77 percent, its peak, in 1964. But then Vietnam, Watergate, and the Iranian hostage crisis delivered such severe blows to the body politic that trust started to plummet—and just kept dropping. In 2011, after years of just a quarter to a third of citizens trusting the government, the percentage declined to a low of 15 percent.

In late 2017, the nonpartisan Pew Research Center reported the trust number at 18 percent of the people surveyed. In the analysis of the data, Pew noted, "Currently, 22% of Republicans and Republican-leaning independents say they can trust government, compared with 15% of Democrats and Democratic leaners. . . . Since the 1970s, trust in government has been consistently higher among members of the party that controls the White House than among the opposition party. However, Republicans have been much more reactive than Democrats to changes in political power. Republicans have expressed much higher levels of trust during Republican than during Democratic presidencies, while Democrats' attitudes have tended to be more consistent, regardless of which party controls the White House." Regardless of party affiliation, voters who lack trust don't have a sense of strong, civic confidence, so they look elsewhere— beyond Washington—for leadership in the White House. Make way for the outsiders.

Besides pointing to the anti-Washington anger now animating a large percentage of the electorate, one can also identify with outsiders' attraction to an optimistic yet (truth be told) naïve hope that a patriotic, put-others-first soul can slay the forces of evil arrayed against good, in what some citizens see as the infested and polluted "swamp" of the nation's capital.

Jefferson Smith, the character played by James Stewart in the 1939 classic film *Mr. Smith Goes to Washington,* personifies the well-meaning and civic-minded amateur attempting to do what's right, despite the machinations of corrupt, conniving political professionals. The conspicuous and noisy antipathy to Washington that exists today produces a deep, inner longing for a modern variation of Jeff Smith, as unrealistic and indisputably romantic as that notion might be and definitely is. Reagan, Clinton, Obama, and Trump all accentuated optimistic visions of the future that appealed to an American past of soaring possibility, harmony among diversity, and unquestioned eminence. Each word in the slogan "Make America Great Again" underscores this point.

Though voters at the presidential level keep picking outsiders for the Oval Office, there's a curious yet intriguing tendency to want differences beyond political party from one chief executive to the next. Carter was the opposite of Ford in background and approach. With his ideological pragmatism and big-picture perspective, Reagan was far different from Carter's cerebral, sweat-each-detail orientation. Verbally agile and an unabashed policy wonk, Clinton wouldn't have been mistaken for either the George Bush he defeated or the George Bush who succeeded him. Obama and George W. Bush would never be confused for the way each handled White House business—and the same observation can be safely advanced comparing Obama and Trump. It's almost as though the US voting public becomes tired of one particular type of leader and, electorally, tries out another figure with an entirely different way of dealing with issues and communicating about policy or other subjects. A persistent about-face attitude toward the way affairs are being conducted accompanies a decision to make a switch—and hope for the best.

Change, in other words, has developed into a constant of the institutional continuity within the presidency during the past several decades, and with that change has come an appetite for fresh, new faces, as mentioned earlier, and a rejection of familiar figures in the American political arena. In the presidency (and to a degree in other high elective offices), the less direct experience one has the better. Amazingly, indeed troublingly, the Oval Office has become the nation's most visible workplace for on-the-job training.

Moreover, the expanded influence of the primaries and caucuses since the 1970s has also had a definite impact on who ultimately became president. Three incumbent chief executives—Ford, Carter, and the elder Bush—faced strong challenges within their own parties (in 1976, 1980, and 1992, respectively), and they all lost in the general election. By contrast, Reagan, Clinton, George W. Bush, and Obama, who did not receive serious competition for renomination, won second terms. If Americans perceive that a president might be vulnerable politically, it signifies possible weakness—and voters never like to imagine weakness in a president, who might have to face an unexpected life-or-death international crisis at 3 o'clock one morning.

Both the Twenty-Second Amendment and the post-1968 reforms in the nominating process have forced those in public life and the citizenry at large to evaluate presidents and White House candidates using data and perspectives that are relatively new in the sweep of US history. Because of the two-term limit, for instance, administrations initiate signature and potentially controversial legislation with a fixed eye on the calendar, if not on the clock. Lyndon Johnson, who served as Senate majority leader before becoming president, once remarked about White House and congressional dynamics, "You've got just one year when they treat you right and before they start worrying about themselves." That's just *one* year out of four—or even eight.

George W. Bush made the Economic Growth and Tax Relief Reconciliation Act of 2001 the centerpiece of his first months in office, and the massive changes in tax rates and rules became law in June 2001. Barack Obama took on health care shortly after becoming president, and the Patient Protection and Affordable Care Act (widely known as "Obamacare") was signed on March 23, 2010, six months after the bill was first advanced in Congress. Donald Trump, who campaigned on a promise to repeal Obamacare, was unable to push a bill through Congress in 2017 that achieved his objective; however, near the end of his first year in office, he signed into law the Tax Cuts and Jobs Act, a staggering piece of legislation that economists estimated would add $1.5 trillion to the nation's debt over a decade. (Not a single Republican voted for Obamacare; not a single Democrat voted for the Tax Cuts and Jobs Act.) In each of these three cases, complicated and contested proposals were agenda items early during these administrations, when a president possesses the most clout.

With the Twenty-Second Amendment, a predictable timetable or schedule has developed. Incoming presidents flex their muscles during the first year, fairly or not referred to as the "honeymoon period." Then concerns related to the congressional midterm elections make major initiatives next to impossible, because neither House members nor senators up for reelection in the midterms are much inclined to tackle legislation that might be costly to their electoral fortunes. After those ballots are counted, presidents focus on winning a second term, which often results in greater concern for political activity than a governing agenda. If a president is reelected, candidates angling to replace the incumbent start throwing their weight around and receive a preponderance of media attention. Politics seems to win out, overwhelming service to the public.

The American cycle of regularly scheduled elections—vastly different from parliamentary democracies, which can schedule confidence votes or call for snap elections—creates a definite pattern of political conduct for both the executive and legislative branches. The last year Obama was president, the Republican-controlled Senate refused to consider Supreme Court nominee Merrick Garland to fill the vacancy resulting from the sudden death of Justice Antonin Scalia. GOP senators argued that the president-to-be, whose inauguration was ten months in the future, should make the selection. Neil Gorsuch was nominated by Trump on January 31, 2017, and confirmed on April 7. The

Republicans got their way, and a president late in his second term appeared to be a limping, if not completely lame, duck. One of the most important presidential powers was politically foreshortened by the legislative branch.

The Twenty-Second Amendment compels a president lucky enough to be elected twice to frontload major policy objectives before political imperatives intervene. Eight years might sound like a long time, and in temporal respects it is. However, when consequential legislation or congressional approval of appointments is considered, there's little doubt that the president has greater political capital in the first year plus, perhaps, a few months—as Johnson tartly observed. Afterward, when a White House is still finding its footing and learning about governing, political factors escalate in importance and, more often than not, take precedence. In addition, midterm voting often reduces a president's legislative advantage in Congress—as happened most recently with Clinton in 1994 (Democrats dropped fifty-four House and eight Senate seats that year), Bush in 2006 (Republicans decreased their numbers in the House by thirty and in the Senate by six), and Obama in 2010 (a loss for Democrats of sixty-three House and six Senate seats). Trump in 2018 benefited from an increase of two GOP senators; however, Democrats flipped control of the House when Republicans dropped forty seats, the largest Democratic gain since the post-Watergate midterm of 1974, when they picked up forty-nine House districts.

Since the ratification of the Twenty-Second Amendment, every president able to seek a full second term—with the sole exception of Johnson—mounted campaigns to remain in office. One wonders whether Eisenhower (the last president born in the nineteenth century and the first constitutionally mandated lame duck) or Reagan would have tried to win a third term if not for term limits. What about Clinton or Obama? (The Gallup Poll's final approval ratings contribute to such speculation: 59 percent for Eisenhower, 63 percent for Reagan, 66 percent for Clinton, and 59 percent for Obama.) Age and health would certainly have been factors in each decision. Reagan at age seventy-seven was the oldest of the four when he left office. Eisenhower was seventy, Clinton fifty-four, and Obama fifty-five. Roosevelt's decision to challenge the two-term tradition and pursue unprecedented third and fourth four-year terms in 1940 and 1944 would have opened the door for his successors from both parties in the 1950s and later. That door, however, was slammed shut when Congress proposed and the states ratified the Twenty-Second Amendment.

It's worth dwelling on the Twenty-Second Amendment and the presidential nominating process that's evolved in recent decades, because each, to varying degrees, has helped determine the nation's highest government official. Term limits rein in the exercise of power; however, they do so at the expense of voters, who no longer have a chance to decide on the continuation of someone the public might judge to be a committed and an effective leader. Was America ready to retire FDR in 1940, with the country still recovering from the Depression and a worldwide conflict beginning to threaten Western civilization in Europe and Asia? Roosevelt garnered 54.7 percent of the popular vote in 1940 and 53.4 percent in 1944, the fourth consecutive majority he received. As touched on previously, the Twenty-Second Amendment was approved by Republican majorities in the House and Senate shortly after the Eightieth Congress assembled in 1947, and its subsequent ratification imposed the time-specific regulation on the presidency—the only elected office on the federal level with such a limitation. Is it fair to the country to mandate an elected official's forced removal from public service, particularly at a time of national crisis?

The current nominating process shifts the selection of major party candidates from Democratic and Republican leaders with expertise in politics and government to grassroots members of each party or, in some cases, to voters interested in participating even without declaring a party affiliation. How complicated is the system we have today? The National Conference of State Legislatures lists five different types of primaries operating across the country in choosing presidential candidates: "closed," "partially closed," "partially open," "open to unaffiliated voters," and "open." Despite the variety of approach state-by-state, the nominating process puts a premium on personality over policy. How an individual *connects* with the public becomes critical, whether in person (with visits, say, to Iowa or New Hampshire) or through the innumerable communication platforms that distribute messages from a candidate or a campaign.

In 2016, sixteen men and one woman vied for the Republican nomination. At times, observers had the feeling that some of the competitors were hoping lightning might strike and ignite their candidacies. As the caucuses and primaries unfolded, Trump's antipolitician, anti-Washington persona appealed to GOP voters, and he secured enough support for the Republican nomination after the Indiana primary on May 3.

For the Democrats that year, Hillary Clinton and Senator Bernie Sanders battled each other from the beginning of February until early June, with Clinton finally ending up with the most delegates. Interestingly, Sanders in defeat took with him a following of supporters afire with political passion that one didn't detect among Clinton backers. When Trump beat Clinton in November, more than a few analysts wondered aloud whether Sanders would have been more appealing to "the forgotten men and women" in Pennsylvania, Michigan, and Wisconsin that put Trump over the top in the Electoral College. Trump and Sanders exemplify the weakening nature of the major parties as political institutions. Most observers date Trump's association with the GOP only back to his questioning of Obama's birth certificate in 2011, while Sanders's official Senate biography identifies him as "the longest serving independent member of Congress in American history," even though he ran for president as a Democrat. Have the parties actually become obsolete or extraneous in the nominating process of the so-called party standard-bearer? Has the candidate-centered process made it more difficult to govern and for a president to work with Congress?

On August 2, 2016, the *New York Times* published a telling graphic that speaks volumes about today's nominating system and the level of involvement by the citizenry. The first image shows that the "United States is home to 324 million people" and that "103 million of them are children, noncitizens or ineligible felons, and they do not have the right to vote." The following box notes that "88 million eligible adults do not vote at all, even in general elections." The next graphic says that "73 million did not vote in the primaries this year." This means, as the following illustration shows, that "60 million people voted in the primaries, and about half chose candidates who eventually dropped out." Text near the bottom of the chart reads, "Just 14 percent of eligible adults—9 percent of the whole nation—voted for either Mr. Trump or Mrs. Clinton. The overall shares were about the same in 2008, the last cycle without an incumbent president running."

The statistics are sobering and also raise serious questions. Do the relatively few primary voters know enough about the candidates to make an informed choice about someone's potential for presidential leadership? Are media images, in either advertisements or news coverage, becoming overriding factors in how the public decides? To what extent are performances in debates with several other candidates, such as those by Republicans in both 2012 and 2016, desirable as occasions to evaluate political and executive prowess? Clearly the nominating procedures that took root in the 1970s have brought figures to the forefront of American politics who would have had trouble receiving a second look in earlier times. Indeed, would Obama, with his limited national experience, have been able to prevail in 2008 had the older rules that emphasized the clout of party officials been in effect? That's highly doubtful. What about Trump in 2016? In earlier times, it's outside the realm of possibility that Republican stalwarts would have tapped someone who engaged in dubious business practices, had no public service experience, and was weakly tied to the GOP as their presidential nominee.

In thinking comprehensively and, yes, critically about the presidency, it's essential to evaluate and assess the individuals involved *and* the forces that shaped those individuals, as well as the office itself. Americans tend to view presidents as a succession of figures, following one after the other in a pageant of "executive Power" (to use the Constitution's phrase again) that helps to unite the nation, especially when crises occur or challenges present themselves. What has been different in recent decades is the rhythm of the White House, including more party changes from one incumbent to the next, more support from outsiders, and more fascination with new political players. That rhythm, punctuated with frequent dissonance, derives from the institutional limits and electoral rules currently in force. Is it time to reconsider who is eligible for the Oval Office and how the White House is won? The chapters that follow take up these questions and their intersecting concerns.

—— T W O ——

Perils of Power

On a January day in 1961, with eight inches of snow from the previous night creating havoc in Washington and a wind chill temperature of seven degrees prompting worry of hypothermia, the just-inaugurated president spoke about a torch. Near the beginning of his inaugural address, John Kennedy said, "Let the word go forth from this time and place, to friend and foe alike, that the torch has been passed to a new generation of Americans." The sentence continued for another fifty-four words, making it one of the longest delivered during that afternoon's oratory. Kennedy uttered the word *generation* (or its plural form) four times in his address. There's a collective promise in this demarcation of time, and what's intriguing is that the slogan for Kennedy's first campaign for Congress in 1946 was "The New Generation Offers a Leader." He must have liked the word and what it evoked.

In the view of the youngest elected president as he succeeded his immediate predecessor, who up to that time had been the oldest, history had reached a hinge point. (As mentioned earlier, Reagan and Trump were both older than Eisenhower when they took office.) Through his rhetoric, with its emphasis on the promise of youth and fresh approaches, Kennedy was making a definite break from the presidents who preceded him, especially Eisenhower, who was born in 1890 and was leaving the White House at age seventy. Kennedy, who entered the world in 1917 and was inaugurated at age forty-three, personified not only a "new generation" of American leaders but also represented a new century.

When you look at the sweep of US history and the relationship of the presidency to each era, it can be similar to trying to solve a puzzle of variously shaped and sized pieces. In the twenty-eight years (seven terms) before Kennedy took office, only three presidents served—Franklin Roosevelt, Harry Truman, and Dwight Eisenhower—each of whom was born during the last two decades of the nineteenth century. By contrast, for the seven terms after Kennedy's assassination, America had six presidents—each born in the twentieth century, on average, within six years of 1917. (Lyndon Johnson was born in 1908, while Jimmy Carter and the senior George Bush were both born in 1924.) Viewing the presidential puzzle from this perspective, the prime question that arises is: What did the "new generation" do with "the torch" as it passed from JFK to LBJ, to Richard Nixon, to Gerald Ford, to Jimmy Carter, to Ronald Reagan, and to George H. W. Bush? During the thirty-two-year period from 1961 to 1993, seven presidents served, six of whom had either tragic or forced endings to their exercise of executive power.

- Kennedy was assassinated in Dallas in 1963.
- Johnson, with his approval ratings languishing in the thirties during much of 1968, decided not to run for reelection that year to avoid being defeated.
- Nixon, who was elected in 1968 and 1972, resigned from office in 1974 in the face of the Watergate scandal and the prospect of impeachment.

- Ford, an unelected and accidental president, lost to Carter in 1976, after narrowly defeating Reagan for the Republican nomination that year.
- Carter, the beneficiary of the anti-Watergate and anti-Nixon mood during 1976, endured the Iranian hostage crisis of 1979 and 1980, before losing reelection in 1980.
- Reagan, the only two-term president between the 1950s and 1990s, was seriously injured in a 1981 assassination attempt and wounded politically during his second term by the Iran-Contra imbroglio, considered by some observers to be an even more substantial scandal than Watergate.
- Bush senior, the first incumbent vice president since Martin Van Buren in 1836 to win a White House campaign, was denied a second term in 1992 by Bill Clinton.

Regrettably, Kennedy's "torch," which had "been passed to a new generation of Americans," more closely resembled a poisoned chalice for the succession of presidents during the three decades after Eisenhower. Remarkably, however, the three presidents who followed Bush senior—Clinton, George W. Bush, and Barack Obama—were each elected twice for four-year terms. Both Clinton and George W. Bush were born in 1946, and Obama in 1961. They represent, if you will, the generation after Kennedy's, a point we'll explore shortly.

Since FDR won his unprecedented four elections in 1932, 1936, 1940, and 1944, eleven incumbent presidents have campaigned to continue as White House residents. Eight won, while three lost—each one of that trio coming from Kennedy's "new generation." The broadcaster and author Tom Brokaw labeled the people who grew up during the Depression, fought in World War II, and then returned to the United States to create an economic and international powerhouse "the Greatest Generation," a superlative phrase that he used as the title for his 1998 best-selling book. At one point early in his book, Brokaw recalls his coverage on NBC of the fiftieth anniversary of D-Day in 1994 and notes, "As I looked over the assembled crowd of veterans, which included everyone from Cabinet officers and captains of industry to retired schoolteachers and machinists, I said, 'I think this is the greatest generation any society has ever produced.' I know this was a bold statement and a sweeping judgment, but since then I have restated it on many occasions. While I am periodically challenged on this premise, I believe I have the facts on my side" (xxx). That might well be the case; however, "the greatest generation"—people born between 1901 and 1924—had difficulties in one particular realm. The presidency, which after World War II amassed greater and greater executive power, also proved during this period to be an office of enormous peril—to one's own life or to one's political existence.

Interestingly, America had endured a similar era of presidential trauma, turbulence, and turnover in the final decades of the nineteenth century. Again, as happened with Kennedy's "new generation," an assassination triggered a cycle that challenged the occupants of America's highest office. Abraham Lincoln was elected twice—in 1860 and 1864—but was shot by John Wilkes Booth on April 14, 1865, five days after the Confederate general Robert E. Lee surrendered at Appomattox.

During the thirty-six years between Lincoln and Theodore Roosevelt (1865–1901), eight men occupied the White House, six of them Republicans. Two of them were assassinated (James Garfield in 1881 and William McKinley in 1901). One, Andrew Johnson, suffered impeachment in 1868. Two secured victories in the Electoral College but did not prevail in the popular vote: Rutherford B. Hayes in 1876 and Benjamin Harrison in 1888. And Grover Cleveland became the only noncontinuous two-term president in US history, winning in 1884, losing in 1888, and coming back to win in 1892. From Lincoln's death to Theodore Roosevelt's ascent, Ulysses S. Grant was the sole traditionally elected two-term president—just as Reagan was in the cluster of Kennedy-generation chief executives.

The aphorism that "history doesn't repeat itself, but it often rhymes" is often attributed to Mark Twain. To a certain extent, we see something resembling a free-verse rhyme scheme in a comparison between US political history in the late nineteenth and the late twentieth centuries. It's almost as though the fatal shootings of Lincoln and Kennedy started chain reactions of presidential problems, resulting in a downward spiral of the office that took years to halt one way or the other. Particularly for the Kennedy generation, what reasons stand out for the travails and tribulations of White House occupants between 1961 and 1993? Were the presidents—three Democrats and four Republicans—seriously flawed people, who contributed to their own difficulties, or were they casualties of the turbulent and tumultuous times during which they served?

In some cases, external forces clearly proved decisive; in others, personal weaknesses were at fault. In certain instances, moreover, two factors conspired together, making effective governing nearly impossible. Nixon, for example, was a shrewd political survivor, who ran on national tickets (for either vice president or president) *five* times over a twenty-year period from 1952 to 1972, a feat that Franklin Roosevelt matched but over a longer span of time. He was also the only political figure other than Thomas Jefferson to serve as vice president before winning two elections to the White House. (Seven other former vice presidents won single terms on their own.) However, besides being intellectually gifted and creative in appealing to voters, he also obsessed about losing power, identifying opponents as "enemies" and sanctioning questionable, if not illegal, measures to suppress what he perceived as threats to that power. On his watch, he had to contend with the Vietnam War and Watergate—and he couldn't survive those debilitating experiences *and* overcome his innate weaknesses. He was forced to resign as impeachment and removal from office loomed not far off in his future.

The 1960s and 1970s were decades of social, cultural, and political upheaval, and the forces that were unleashed possessed such intensity that the 1980s, though less explosive, continued to reflect what one commentator referred to as "the passions of the Republic." By its nature and position, the White House is always at the center of whatever storm is buffeting the nation. International danger. Racial injustice. Economic malaise. Gender inequity. Sexual repression. The years spanning Kennedy to Bush senior encompassed revolution, war, and most everything in between—with the presidents forced to cope with problems they were dealt but never could have predicted.

Moreover, the attitude and approach of the news media after Vietnam and Watergate changed dramatically. Reporters saw themselves more as investigators and less as stenographers. Gone were the days of shielding a president's physical disability or sexual indiscretion from the public. Now, though politicians didn't like it, personal matters became fair game for journalists to scrutinize and probe. As a result, the office became less majestic, as citizens learned about presidential lies concerning war and criminality related to a reelection campaign. News organizations established new rules for coverage, and in some cases the posture was that anything goes.

In chapter 1, we looked at the consequences of the Twenty-Second Amendment on the presidency and the individual figures who occupy the White House. The two-term limit can lead to the loss of political acuity by the president and those surrounding the presidency, and a day or so after winning reelection, chatter begins about the lame duck status of the leader of the free world. That talk, inevitably, becomes louder with each passing day, a subject to which we return in chapter 5.

Another, even more recent constitutional amendment has had a direct impact on the hierarchy of the executive branch. First considered in the aftermath of the Kennedy assassination, the Twenty-Fifth Amendment addresses presidential succession when an incumbent is "unable to discharge the powers and duties" related to the office, and it also specifies that a president can select a new vice president should that position become vacant for whatever reason. Majority votes in both the House and the Senate are required to confirm the new number 2. On sixteen different occasions before this amendment was ratified, the position of vice president was not occupied, and seven times the vacancy lasted almost an entire four-year term. Incredibly, between September 19, 1881, and March 4, 1889—nearly seven and a half years!—the United States had a vice president for only 266 days, because President James Garfield was assassinated in 1881, and Vice President Thomas Hendricks died in office in 1885.

The Twenty-Fifth Amendment was proposed by Congress on July 6, 1965, and ratified on February 10, 1967. If it had not existed after the resignations of Vice President Spiro Agnew on bribery charges in 1973 and Nixon for everything under the rubric of Watergate in 1974, then-Speaker of the House Carl Albert, a Democrat, would have succeeded the Republican Nixon as president. Indeed, Gerald Ford would have remained a member of the House of Representatives—and he would never have been either vice president or president. It's legitimate to wonder whether the Democratic President Albert would have taken on the Republican Ronald Reagan in 1976. Could any Republican in that year have overcome the lingering hostility toward Nixon? For Democrats, would Jimmy Carter have challenged a sitting president from his party, had Albert sought to continue as president? The Twenty-Fifth Amendment made those questions unnecessary, and, as it turned out, Albert decided not to seek reelection to his House seat in 1976.

The presidents we identify as members of the greatest generation couldn't seem to avoid institution-shaking problems and predicaments that affected them personally and politically. By contrast, the winners of the White House from the baby boomer generation—women and men born between 1946 and 1964—seem to have greater longevity in office or more acutely developed survival skills. As mentioned previously, from 1993 until 2017, the United States has had three consecutive two-term presidents: Bill Clinton, George W. Bush, and Barack Obama. The only other period in this nation's history with a trio of consecutive two-term victors occurred at the beginning of the nineteenth century. Thomas Jefferson, James Madison, and James Monroe each prevailed twice and ultimately served eight years in the presidency. From March 4, 1801, to March 4, 1825, Jefferson, Madison, and Monroe engaged in what could be described accurately as the friendly transfer of executive authority. During that quarter century, Jefferson, Madison, and Monroe were standard-bearers of the Democratic-Republican Party. The three men knew each other well; each served several years as secretary of state, and they all came from Virginia. Back then, the United States was settling down and establishing itself as a new nation. Continuity in leadership among Democratic and Republican comrades brought a sense of stability to the presidency after the hurly-burly of the revolution and founding.

Despite the coincidence of their having repeated the sequence of three straight two-term presidents, it would be difficult to find three more dissimilar figures than Clinton, Bush, and Obama. More than geography and political experience differentiate the centrist Clinton, the conservative Bush, and the more liberal Obama. Interestingly, each served as president amid party-switching elections on the congressional level in 1994, 2006, and 2010. Not once during the triumvirate of Jefferson, Madison, and Monroe did the House or Senate shift from the Democratic-Republican Party of the incumbent president.

As it happened, the 1824 election that followed the three straight two-term presidencies was settled by a vote in the House of Representatives, because no candidate received the 131 Electoral College votes needed to win that year. Four members of the Democratic-Republican Party—John Quincy Adams, Andrew Jackson, William Crawford, and Henry Clay—so divided voter allegiances across the country's twenty-four states that each won substantial Electoral College support. Jackson, who won the popular vote by more than 10 percent, garnered 99 electoral votes to 84 for Adams, 41 for Crawford, and 37 for Clay. In the House's election, one vote for each state, Clay's backing of Adams—memorably christened and criticized as a "corrupt bargain" because Clay was later appointed secretary of state—made the son of the second president (John Adams) the sixth US president. Both Adamses, however, lost their reelection campaigns. In 1828, Jackson, now running as just a "Democrat," easily defeated the "National Republican" Adams, bringing an end to the succession of two-term chief executives.

History never repeats itself in every particular, but one wonders about parallels and circumstances related to the elections of 1824 and 2016, each of which followed a trio of two termers and resulted in the loser of the popular vote being inaugurated. What happened as a result of the 1824 election—the House's operating under the provisions of the Twelfth Amendment proving decisive—was unprecedented. But so, too, was the situation in 2016 of someone without any government experience assuming the highest office in the federal government. Will 2020 continue and expand the two-term trend, or will it be like 1828, which started a new, more participatory politics in America?

Donald Trump was born in 1946, the same year as Clinton and the junior Bush, and the only year in US history to produce three presidents. Starting with Clinton's victory in 1992, the presidential pendulum has swung between the Democratic Party and the Republican Party four times. Amid such change, three straight two termers have won reelection and served the full eight years, raising questions concerning why and whether Trump might be the fourth consecutive White House occupant to complete the allowable time to serve as set by the Twenty-Second Amendment.

Has the presidency become so powerful that an incumbent's advantage is now too great to overcome, especially in terms of fund-raising? Were the citizens who went to the polls across the country—the average turnout for the three presidential elections from 1996, 2004, and 2012 with an incumbent running was 53.5 percent, according to Federal Election Commission figures—reluctant to register a vote of "no confidence" in the nation's leader, especially at a time of turmoil at home and abroad? Were Clinton, Bush, and Obama beneficiaries of generally weak opponents, who had serious difficulties exciting the base voters of their parties, as was the case with Bob Dole in 1996, John Kerry in 2004, and Mitt Romney in 2012?

Though Clinton, the younger Bush, and Obama completed two terms, each faced perilous episodes during their presidencies. Clinton, in fact, became the only elected president in history ever to be impeached by the House of Representatives. (Andrew Johnson was impeached in 1868, but he was Lincoln's vice president and succeeded Lincoln after the assassination.) Clinton was impeached on December 19, 1998, for perjury and obstruction of justice related to an extramarital affair. Interestingly, the same month the House voted two articles of impeachment, Clinton recorded his highest approval rating as president—73 percent—as measured by a Gallup opinion survey. (Six months into his first term, in June 1993, Clinton's approval was half that, at 37 percent.) He was acquitted in a Senate trial and left the White House with an average of 55.1 percent of those polled approving his work as president, again according to Gallup. Both Bush and Obama were under 50 percent approval in their eight-year Gallup averages: Bush at 49.4 percent and Obama at 47.9 percent. To show the volatility of public opinion, Bush reached 90 percent approval right after the terrorist attack on September 11, 2001—and dropped to 25 percent with the financial crisis in October 2008. Obama departed the White House in 2017 with 59 percent approval, but he had weathered several months between 40 and 42 percent in 2011, 2013, and 2014. Strikingly, in 2000, 2008, and 2016, respectively, Clinton, Bush, and Obama all failed to have a nominee from his own party replace him.

Modern-day presidents (for the sake of our argument, the dozen since ratification of the Twenty-Second Amendment) govern in different political, cultural, social, and economic environments from the thirty-two figures who preceded them. Yet even in its earliest days, the office evoked woe-is-me declarations from the nation's leaders. In an April 1, 1789, letter to Henry Knox, George Washington, who became the first president on April 30 of that year, wrote, "My movements to the chair of government will be accompanied by feelings not unlike those of a culprit who is going to the place of his execution; so unwilling am I, in the evening of a life nearly consumed in public cares, to quit a peaceful abode for an Ocean of difficulties, without that competency of political skill, abilities & inclination which is necessary to manage the helm." After learning that his son John Quincy Adams would become the sixth president in 1825, the second one—John Adams—remarked, "No man who ever held the office of President would congratulate a friend on obtaining it." As mentioned in the prologue, while serving as vice president under John Adams, Thomas Jefferson seemed to dismiss the prospect of "succession to the President's chair," saying, "The second office of this government is honorable & easy, the first is but a splendid misery."

These quotations from the first three presidents set the tone for other statements, written or spoken, of discontent and frustration by subsequent chief executives. For Andrew Jackson, himself an owner of slaves, serving as president was "dignified slavery." Woodrow Wilson, like Jackson a two termer, saw his lofty position this way: "The office of President requires the constitution of an athlete, the patience of a mother, and the endurance of an early Christian. . . . The President is a superior kind of slave." Between Jackson and Wilson, James A. Garfield expressed his annoyance at his White House duty: "My God! What is there in this place that a man should ever want to get into it?" Though not known for memorable statements, Calvin Coolidge wrote in a letter to his father, "I suppose I am the most powerful man in the world, but great power does not mean much except great limitations. I cannot have any freedom even to go and come. I am only in the clutch of forces that are greater than I am." As a five-year-old boy, Franklin Roosevelt met Grover Cleveland in the White House during Cleveland's first term. The twenty-second (and subsequently the twenty-fourth) US chief executive patted his visitor on the head, declaring, "My little man, I am making a strange wish for you. It is that you may never be President of the United States." Harry Truman once remarked, "Being a president is like riding a tiger. A man has to keep on riding or be swallowed." The plain-speaking

Missourian considered the White House "the great white jail," and Clinton expanded on that image to call the residence and offices at 1600 Pennsylvania Avenue "the crown jewel of the Federal penitentiary system." Lyndon Johnson gave new meaning to the title of the official presidential anthem, "Hail to the Chief," when he observed, "Being president is like being a jackass in a hailstorm. There's nothing to do but stand there and take it."

More than anything, such observations emphasizing circumscription and exasperation—and you could fill several additional pages with comparable ones—capture the irritation of strong-willed, ego-driven individuals facing life-and-death responsibilities and institutionally imposed isolation. Choreographed public ceremonies might take a president anywhere in America or the world in grand style, but lonely decision making always awaits offstage away from probing cameras. No matter the quality of the cabinet or the staff, the final judgment on the most significant matters comes down to the conclusion and call of one person.

James Buchanan, who served right before Lincoln and failed to take measures to avert the Civil War, legitimately occupies the bottommost place in an array of presidential rankings by historians and political scientists. Yet with these facts duly noted, John Kennedy spoke truth about power and its complexities when he told Lincoln scholar David Herbert Donald in 1962, "No one has a right to grade a President—not even poor James Buchanan—who has not sat in his chair, examined the mail and information that came across his desk, and learned why he made his decisions" (*Lincoln,* 13). Only one person sits in "the chair of government" (to use Washington's phrase) at a time.

That chair, though, is surrounded by an ever-increasing number of staff members. At the beginning of the nineteenth century, Jefferson had one secretary and one messenger to assist him, whose salaries he personally paid. A century later, McKinley worked with a staff of fifteen to twenty, according to the White House Historical Association. As the twenty-first century started, the Executive Office of the president (in this case that of George W. Bush) had mushroomed to between two thousand and twenty-five hundred men and women in policy-making roles of one kind or another. The current statistics symbolize the expansion of White House power and authority, especially during the decades after World War I.

Theodore Roosevelt, memorably described as a "steam engine in trousers," once said, "While president, I have been president emphatically." He dramatized himself and the office, making Americans view executive leadership differently than ever before. The highest-elected figure in the nation's government possessed what he called a "bully pulpit" to focus public attention not only on a president's agenda but also on the president as a person. Though a skilled writer and voracious reader—pursuits generally conducted in solitude—TR used his "pulpit" with greater frequency and more energetically than any turn-of-the-century, circuit-riding preacher. He benefited, too, from the new, emerging technology of motion or moving pictures, which rendered him in action and dramatized "the strenuous life" he advocated.

Democrat Woodrow Wilson, who was elected in 1912 with only 41.8 percent of the popular vote, benefited that year from Roosevelt's third-party challenge to the reelection bid of the incumbent Republican president, William Howard Taft. TR, who had handpicked Taft to succeed him four years earlier, just couldn't restrain himself. He was fifty-four at the time and wanted *his* pulpit back, proving the veracity of the quip that the only cure for the presidential virus is embalming fluid. Incredibly, Roosevelt returned to the GOP fold in 1916 and wanted the party's presidential nomination, though it went to Supreme Court Justice Charles Evans Hughes.

Wilson narrowly defeated Hughes—but for a second time failed to capture 50 percent of the popular vote. One of Wilson's supporters suggested the slogan "He Kept Us Out of War," which the commander in chief succeeded in doing until he asked Congress for a declaration of war against Germany less than a month after his second inauguration in 1917. US participation in the Great War and the subsequent Paris Peace Conference in 1919 expanded the military and diplomatic influence of the presidency and also brought into sharper focus the perception that America was emerging as a dominant player on the world stage.

To illustrate what US involvement in those European hostilities meant over a century ago, Wilson concluded one of his speeches championing the postwar Treaty of Versailles and the establishment of the League of Nations with this stirring statement:

> My fellow citizens, let us—every one of us—bind ourselves in a solemn league and covenant of our own that we will redeem the expectation of the world, that we will not allow any man to stand in the way of it, that the world shall hereafter bless and not curse us, that the world hereafter shall follow us and not turn aside from us, and that in leading we will not lead along the paths of private advantage, we will not lead along the paths of national ambition, but we will be proud and happy to lead along the path of right, so that men shall always say that American soldiers saved Europe and American citizens saved the world. (Portland, Oregon, September 15, 1919)

Global leadership, moral example, salvation of others: it's all there, directly from the mouth of the president in a rhetorical eruption of 121 words in one sentence. As it turned out, of course, the Senate failed to approve the treaty (and Wilson suffered a debilitating stroke while seeking its ratification)—perils of the presidency both in terms of policy and personal health—but American primacy in international affairs had become a fact of twentieth-century life and increased the dangers for anyone occupying the Oval Office.

According to the official statistics of the Department of Veterans Affairs, from the time the United States declared war on

April 6, 1917, until the Armistice on November 11, 1918, a total of 4,734,991 service members became involved in World War I. By contrast, 16,112,566 participated in the American military during World War II, for which combat lasted nearly four years. Like his distant cousin Theodore, who directly appealed to Wilson without success to join the fighting forces in Europe, Franklin Roosevelt enlarged the purview of the presidency, stretching its authority and activity with almost daily regularity.

Even before he won his first term by defeating the incumbent Herbert Hoover in 1932, FDR knew the approach he wanted to pursue in dealing with the devastation of the Great Depression. "The country needs and, unless I mistake its temper, the country demands bold, persistent experimentation," he proclaimed in a commencement address at Oglethorpe University in May 1932. "It is common sense to take a method and try it: If it fails, admit it frankly and try another. But above all, try something." As president, Roosevelt used the federal government boldly, first in responding to the Depression and then in mounting the American war effort for the Allies to fight the Axis powers in Europe, Asia, Africa, and elsewhere.

Sometimes, however, FDR reached too far in trying to expand the role of the executive branch and found himself cornered in difficult, if not perilous, circumstances. Sixteen days after his second inauguration in 1937, he announced a proposal to add as many as six new justices to the Supreme Court, ostensibly to enhance judicial efficiency. Commentators interpreted the initiative as an attempt "to pack" the highest court with judges agreeable to FDR's policies and legislation. Ultimately, the reorganization plan was never approved by Congress, but Washington and the nation came to understand the extent to which this president was willing to exert pressure on another branch of the federal government. The war years—and two more reelection victories—boosted the president's already healthy sense of command, but peril lurked at nearly every turn.

Roosevelt's efforts to expand executive power and lengthen the time-honored two terms of service established by George

Washington through his personal, yet informal, precedent made Americans and citizens in other countries view the presidency differently than ever before. FDR forcefully changed the presidency—but after his death there was a formal return to the established tradition. For better or for worse, ratification of the Twenty-Second Amendment was one, potent, reactive measure to impose definite limits on the occupant of the White House. In a tripartite system of government that emphasizes the sharing of powers, seeking balance is a perpetual concern—and worry—for those involved in exercising authority.

In 1956, at the midpoint of Eisenhower's eight years as president, Clinton Rossiter's acute institutional analysis *The American Presidency* appeared. One observation describes the position of the chief executive in the post-FDR context as follows:

> The President is not a Gulliver immobilized by ten thousand tiny cords, nor even a Prometheus chained to a rock of frustration. He is, rather, a kind of magnificent lion who can roam widely and do great deeds so long as he does not try to break loose from his broad reservation. Our pluralistic system of restraints is designed to keep him from going out of bounds, not to paralyze him in the field that has been reserved for his use. He will feel few checks upon his power if he uses that power as he should. This may well be the final definition of the strong and successful President: the one who knows just how far he can go in the direction he wants to go. If he cannot judge the limits of his power, he cannot call upon its strength. If he cannot sense the possible, he will exhaust himself attempting the impossible. (72–73)

Less than a decade later, in the summer of 1964, Congress passed the Gulf of Tonkin resolution authorizing Lyndon Johnson to escalate US military involvement in Vietnam. Throughout more than eight years of war in Southeast Asia, there was never a formal war declaration by Congress. Mission creep quickly became a crowded and violent slog for the nearly 3.5 million American service members deployed there. The political and social consequences proved serious enough that Johnson, a landslide victor in the 1964 election, decided he didn't want to chance a reelection run four years later. His successor, Richard Nixon, also wrestled with Vietnam throughout his five-and-a-half years in the White House, and from June 1972, Watergate began to metastasize, eventually leading to the disgrace of resignation on August 8, 1974.

In 1973, the historian Arthur M. Schlesinger Jr., who had personal White House experience during the Kennedy years, examined the nation's highest office and drew conclusions far different from Rossiter's. The "magnificent lion" had indeed tried "to break loose from his broad reservation," creating, in Schlesinger's judgment, a "runaway presidency" with an "expansion and abuse of presidential power." Schlesinger called his study *The Imperial Presidency*, a phrase of unavoidable resonance and pertinence as the misdeeds and malfeasance of the Nixon administration multiplied in front of congressional committees, before federal judges, and within the pages of newspapers, most prominently the *Washington Post*.

The Vietnam War and Watergate exposed to full public view the enormous perils a president faces by pushing executive power beyond acceptable institutional and legal bounds. Both Johnson and Nixon paid the highest possible political price: the conclusion of their presidencies before they intended to leave office. Still, understanding the boundaries of the office escaped Nixon's considerable intelligence even after he vacated the White House. In 1977, he told interviewer David Frost, "When the president does it, that means that it is not illegal."

Congress, however, reacted by passing legislation aimed at erecting fences a leonine leaper would have trouble clearing. The War Powers Act in 1973, the Budget and Impoundment Control Act in 1974, the Independent Counsel Act in 1978, and the Foreign Intelligence Surveillance Act the same year put new, formal "checks" of one kind or another—and with varying success—on what a president could do in certain situations. In addition to Congress, the Supreme Court decided cases (e.g., *United States v. Nixon* in 1974 and *Clinton v. Jones* in 1997) that questioned arguments about executive privilege and presidential immunity. More fences erected by another branch of government were going up. And, of course, Clinton was himself impeached by the House in late 1998.

However, not long after the terrorist attacks on September 11, 2001, and the decision by George W. Bush to send the US military into combat, first in Afghanistan and then in Iraq, the White House began once again to flex executive-branch muscles not really used since the 1970s. The Bush administration's "War on Terror" became a twenty-first-century example of an observation about fluctuating power in US government made memorably by Alexis de Tocqueville in the first volume of *Democracy in America* (1835). In a section titled "Accidental Causes That May Increase the Influence of Executive Power," he wrote, "If the Union's existence were constantly menaced, and if its great interests were continually interwoven with those of other powerful nations, one would see the prestige of the executive growing, because of what was expected from it and of what it did" (114). More than "the prestige of the executive" became involved in the reaction to September 11, complete with the preemptive (and still justifiably controversial) war in Iraq.

In analysis with back-to-the-future intimations, Schlesinger, in fact, noted parallels in US history that he had previously explored when Nixon occupied the White House. Emphasizing the secrecy surrounding the Bush administration, Schlesinger wrote in *War and the American Presidency* (2004) that "the impact of 9/11 and of the overhanging terrorist threat gives more power than ever to the imperial presidency and places the separation of powers ordained by the Constitution under unprecedented, and at times unbearable, strain" (66). Bush served a full eight years as president, but his approval ratings never reached 40 percent throughout his last two years, according to

Gallup surveys. His first term average of 62 percent approval was the highest since Johnson's of 74 percent, and LBJ's term was abbreviated (November 1963 until January 1965) because he assumed the presidency after Kennedy's assassination.

One definite conclusion can be drawn from recent history: nothing is less permanent or more unpredictable than presidential fortunes, especially at a time of voter volatility and media multiplicity. In both 2008 and 2012, Obama received over 50 percent of the popular vote; however, his average approval ratings computed by Gallup after his first and second terms didn't reach the 50 percent mark in either case.

Early in his still-illuminating study *Presidential Power* (1960), Richard E. Neustadt quotes a famous lament of Truman: "I sit here all day trying to persuade people to do the things they ought to have sense enough to do without my persuading them. . . .That's all the powers of the President amount to." In the next paragraph, Neustadt distills Truman's vituperative observation into the scholar's most famous epigram: "Presidential *power* is the power to persuade" (9–10; italics in the original). Those seven words immediately show the significance of making compelling, informed arguments to members of Congress, appointees in the executive branch, foreign leaders, journalists, and the people at large in whatever setting the chief executive might be. Effective communication persuades, resulting in committed followership and political support; the opposite provokes questions and doubts that impede or prevent the acceptance of a proposal or policy. Power means addition and multiplication—and *not* subtraction or division—and that power, in large measure, derives from a message with a deliberate meaning and objective. A certain trumpet, in other words.

Nietzsche in *Thus Spoke Zarathustra* sketches a picture of a tightrope performer attempting to cross "a rope over an abyss." That image—a tightrope walker balancing above a craggy abyss, completely alone, always in peril, with a long way still to navigate—could substitute for the formal portrait of every president. Besides the ability to persuade, maintaining one's equilibrium is essential but never easy. Successful presidential performance is a nonstop tightrope walk to reach a steadying stability between principle and pragmatism, between domestic concerns and international affairs, between traditional practices and new initiatives, between statecraft and stagecraft, between governing and campaigning, between appealing to the public at large and wooing a partisan base, between transparency and secrecy, and so on.

There's a hint of regret in Theodore Roosevelt's observation that "if there is not the great occasion, you don't get the great statesman; if Lincoln had lived in times of peace, no one would know his name now." But we do know Lincoln's name. We also know Washington's name, and we know Franklin Roosevelt's name—the three most highly rated presidents in US history, according to the most authoritative rankings of White House occupants involving scholars in history and political science. Interestingly, Washington, Lincoln, and FDR served, respectively, during the eighteenth, nineteenth, and twentieth centuries, at times the republic was undergoing strenuous tests: the Revolution and founding years, the Civil War, and the Great Depression and World War II. Will there be a twenty-first-century addition to this presidential pantheon? What will be, in TR's phrase, "the great occasion" that triggers historic leadership? Prophecy, with the objective of clairvoyance, and history-based political analysis mix together like oil and water—each substance naturally separating from the other.

What we do know is that the American presidency is without challenge the most resilient and potentially transformative office in a system emphasizing checks and balances, power sharing, and constant tension among the other branches of government. Executing the metaphorical tightrope walk always involves potential peril—but a triumphant performance can bring with it national progress and even greater possibilities for the United States and for the world.

—— THREE ——

Paralysis of Polarization

When Congress passed legislation creating Medicare and Medicaid in 1965, 13 (of 32) Republican senators joined 57 Democratic colleagues in the final roll call that approved the two amendments to the Social Security Act of 1935. The day before, half of the House Republicans—70 of 140—voted in favor of the federal insurance programs for older and poorer Americans, with 237 of 293 Democratic members also saying "yea."

Forty-five years later in 2010, after the House and Senate debated the Patient Protection and Affordable Care Act, not a single Republican in either chamber on Capitol Hill supported that bill. One of the first bills Republicans pushed after regaining control of the House in 2011 carried this title: Repealing the Job-Killing Health Care Law Act (H.R.2). Every House Republican voted for repeal, beginning a series of failed GOP attempts at overturning the legislation that continued throughout the next six years Barack Obama occupied the White House. As time passed, the designation "Obamacare," which began as an epithet coined by conservative media, became unobjectionable— even to Obama and his administration—and it developed into the term most often used in referring to the program.

What had happened in American political life between the presidencies of Lyndon Johnson and Barack Obama to increase and intensify partisanship in Washington to such a degree? Had members of the two major parties abandoned their positions near the political center to occupy more ideological territory on the extremes, either left or right? Was lockstep polarization, even political tribalism, replacing partisan yet practicable give-and-take to the point at which charges of dysfunction began to be heard with almost daily frequency, and government shut-downs occurred with increasing regularity?

After the presidential election of 1964 (a year before Medicare and Medicaid passed), the US political map began to look decidedly different from those of the past. Johnson lost five southern states to his GOP opponent, Senator Barry Goldwater of Arizona: Alabama, Georgia, Louisiana, Mississippi, and South Carolina. Throughout the previous century—since Abraham Lincoln's election as the first Republican president and the post–Civil War Reconstruction days—the South was so reliably Democratic that citizens residing below the Mason-Dixon Line were often called "Yellow Dog Democrats," meaning that, according to regional lore, they preferred to cast their votes for any yellowish old cur rather than vote for a Republican. Even John Kennedy, a northern Catholic Democrat, had carried most of Dixie four years earlier.

Johnson, who as the vice-presidential running mate helped Kennedy win the South (especially Texas), attributed the rise of Republican fortunes in 1964 to enactment of that year's Civil Rights Act, outlawing employment discrimination and segregation in public places. In fact, shortly after signing the landmark bill on July 2, LBJ told one of his assistants, "I think we just delivered the South to the Republican Party for a long time to come." Except for George Wallace, once and future Alabama governor (over sixteen years in office) and winner of five southern states as a third-party presidential candidate in 1968, and Jimmy Carter, a former Georgia governor, who carried the South for Democrats in 1976, Johnson's prediction has proved largely true. A national policy initiative to confront prejudice and racism had enduring regional political consequences.

Interestingly, in the actual congressional vote for the Civil Rights Act of 1964, Republican support in the House was 76 percent, compared to 60 percent of Democrats. In the Senate, 82 percent of Republicans backed the legislation compared with 69 percent of Democrats. Though the seeds of significant change were planted in southern soil, a bipartisan approach, which was also seen to a lesser degree with Medicare and Medicaid in 1965, continued for several years before Congress began to act with more pronounced party unity, rather than with the cross-party activity that previously existed. Both major parties used to be more diverse and heterogeneous, with Democrats combining conservative southerners with liberal, urban northerners. Republicans boasted moderate, even in some cases liberal, officeholders in the North and throughout the Midwest, along with some conservatives, mainly in sunny climes. Each party featured a wide spectrum of political viewpoints.

The two main parties nowadays are more recognizably regional, ideologically homogenous, and pointedly partisan. The Northeast and West Coast are, by and large, Democratic strongholds, while the South and Southwest have become predominantly Republican domains. The large maps projected by television networks on November election nights every four years reflect what has happened geographically with bright red and blue states.

Of course, there's a danger in overgeneralizing. Most congressional districts in the South or Southwest are decidedly Republican; however, gerrymandering to create minority-defined legislative seats also takes place after each census. In some cases, the district lines encompassing areas populated by African Americans or Hispanics look like they might have been drawn by a first grader without, to be kind, any sense of artistic control. Sophisticated computer programs now allow people involved in drawing district lines to know the demographic and political composition with such precision that, it is remarked with justification, politicians today choose their voters rather than voters choosing their political representatives.

In 2014, the nonpartisan Pew Research Center conducted an extensive study of political polarization (Political Polarization in the American Public: How Increasing Ideological Uniformity and Partisan Antipathy Affect Politics, Compromise and Everyday Life) comparing its prevalence in the past with contemporary times. As recently as the 1970s, there existed (in Pew's phrase) "substantial overlap" between the most conservative and the most liberal members of Congress in both parties. Each succeeding decade in this analysis reflects decline in the overlap, and by 2011–12 "there was no overlap at all in either chamber." Political scientists who interpreted this data and other studies concluded their evaluation of all the roll call votes they consulted with this judgment, "Congress is now more polarized than at any time since the end of Reconstruction."

The consequences of this polarization are profound and institutionally influential on the presidency. Bipartisan consensus, let alone compromise that satisfies members of both parties, often seems impossible, as we saw with the Affordable Care Act and the multiple unsuccessful efforts to repeal it in recent years. After the ACA, or Obamacare, became law, Republican House members made over sixty legislative attempts to repeal it. With less inclination to work across the aisle, members of the House and Senate find themselves spending more of their time with like-minded political figures and supporters. Opponents occupy different—and distant, if not alien—territory. Having a rarely-the-twain-shall-meet situation for the two camps can mean that the most partisan activists on either side become the most heard and followed in certain situations. The greater the emphasis on the extremes, conservative or liberal, the less we see any attempt to arrive at a political midpoint, what might be considered an animating center, that brings together the best thinking from the left and the right in a dynamic synthesis of the contesting viewpoints.

The relative absence of bipartisanship leads to legitimate complaints of political paralysis and governmental dysfunction. Moreover, on a personal, one-on-one level, civility and comity decline, too. Knifelike statements always seem at the ready to wound the president or an opposing legislator. Two lines from W. B. Yeats's poem "The Second Coming" describe a time when extremes dominate without an anchoring midpoint: "Things fall apart; the centre cannot hold; Mere anarchy is loosed upon the world." Contemporary American politics often resembles the image Yeats's words convey and the frustrations so many citizens feel when they watch or read about Washington's antics, which the nation's first leaders could never have envisaged. Indeed, back in 1780, John Adams wrote in a letter, "There is nothing which I dread so much as a division of the republic into two great parties, each arranged under its leader, and concerting measures in opposition to each other." The future president considered two-party division "the greatest political evil" to the principles and system of government then taking shape in the minds of the founders.

Since Johnson's prediction in 1964, the shift in direction toward more partisanship and greater polarization has been relatively gradual yet undeniable. However, a turning point for each party occurred during the summer of 1987. Razor-sharp Democratic and Republican daggers came out of the pockets of tailored suits to destroy political opponents, and in both cases the attacks ultimately proved fatal. American politics had arrived at a point at which the return to authentic bonhomie among electoral competitors had become rare, if not impossible.

In July 1987, President Reagan nominated Robert Bork—a federal appeals court judge, who as acting attorney general in Nixon's Justice Department had fired Watergate special prosecutor Archibald Cox in 1973—to the US Supreme Court. Senate Democrats, then in the majority, hadn't forgotten the jurist's association with Nixon and decided to kill Bork's chances, calling him "a right-wing loony" and an "extreme ideological activist." Indeed, the pitched battle over this judicial nomination became so intense that a new word entered the vocabulary. According to no less an authority than the *Oxford English Dictionary*, the verb "to bork" means "to defame or vilify [a person] systematically, especially in the mass media, usually with the aim of preventing his or her appointment to public office." The borking of Bork worked. In October of that year, the Senate voted fifty-eight to forty-two not to confirm him. A month later, Anthony Kennedy was nominated and received a vote of ninety-seven to zero for confirmation.

At precisely the time Democrats were attacking Bork—and it is probably less a historical coincidence than a convergence of similarly motivated (and malevolent) intentions—Newt Gingrich, a Republican House member, began plotting to undermine and overthrow the Democratic Speaker of the House, Jim Wright, for what Gingrich considered questionable ethics practices. The first Republican to represent the Sixth Congressional District of Georgia, Gingrich was in his fifth term in 1987 and already recognized for the incendiary rhetoric he directed at political opponents.

In his memoir, *Lessons Learned the Hard Way* (1998), Gingrich writes, "The decisive moment for me came in August 1987. . . . Borrowing from Lincoln's formulation that a house divided—half-slave and half-free—cannot stand, I came to the conviction that America could not be half-corrupt and half-honest. One culture or the other would have to win" (92–93). Not quite two years later, Wright became the first Speaker to resign amid scandal, leaving office after a protracted investigation, spearheaded by Gingrich, that focused on bulk purchases of books to boost speaking fees. By the time Wright quit, Gingrich had become the GOP's minority whip, and in 1995, after the Republican Revolution in the 1994 midterm elections put Republicans in the House and Senate majorities for the first time since 1953, Gingrich himself became Speaker. By then, his political tactics, which shared the techniques and objectives advanced by the Democrats in the condemnation of Bork, had become commonplace. Brass-knuckled partisanship was de rigueur—at least for ambitious Washington players—and presidents increasingly had to deal with the consequences, often playing without the political equivalent of the Marquis of Queensberry rules. Opponents were now often perceived as enemies, and eliminating them, in whatever manner and at whatever cost, became paramount. America had arrived at a political turning point.

Just before the problems of Bork and Wright became partisan obsessions in 1987, revelations of Gary Hart's alleged marital infidelity stunned the political world and signaled how far the news media would go in reporting about the private life of a presidential aspirant. Hart's fall from potential 1988 Democratic frontrunner to former candidate took exactly twenty-six days: he announced on April 13, 1987, and withdrew on May 8. On Sunday, May 3, the *Miami Herald* reported that Hart "spent Friday night and most of Saturday in his Capitol Hill townhouse with a young woman who flew from Miami and met him." Three days later, at a press conference in New Hampshire, a *Washington Post* correspondent directly asked the former Colorado senator, "Have you ever committed adultery?" Though Hart responded he didn't think it was "a fair question," his candidacy collapsed, ending forty-eight hours later. Since the 1970s, the news media had become more inclined to probe the accuracy of a politician's projected image, and this new concern would turn into a partisan weapon a decade after Hart's demise.

The impeachment of Bill Clinton in 1998, mentioned in the last chapter, is instructive about the private becoming public, and it is also a case study of the divergence of opinion we now see between elected politicians and the voters who elect them. Republicans in the House, spearheaded once again by Gingrich, made the prospect of presidential impeachment a central issue of that year's midterm elections. Yet instead of gaining House seats, as usually occurs for the party not controlling the White

House, the GOP dropped five seats, and Gingrich decided to resign as Speaker and as a House member a few days after that year's Election Day. What's revealing is that Clinton's highest job approval rating over his two terms in office, as measured by Gallup, reached 73 percent on December 19–20, 1998, with just 25 percent disapproving. The House formally impeached Clinton on charges of perjury and obstruction of justice on December 19. During the trial in the Senate—from January 7, until February 12, 1999—Clinton's job approval averaged 67.6 percent. Interestingly, the next month, after he was acquitted by the Senate, his job rating started to decline and never again reached the heights of late 1998 or early 1999.

The American people, as measured by public opinion surveys, were registering their opposition to the blatantly partisan impeachment by the House and the president's possible removal from office in a Senate trial. A *New York Times*/CBS News poll, which was released on December 21, 1998, was almost identical to Gallup's, noting that 72 percent approved of the job Clinton was doing. In the *Times* article about the survey, Adam Nagourney and Michael R. Kagay wrote that the "poll suggests that almost a year after the initial reports of Mr. Clinton's relationship with Monica S. Lewinsky, the public continues to be almost completely at odds with much of Washington's political establishment over the impact and significance of Mr. Clinton's affair, and attempts by an independent counsel and Republicans in Congress to prove he tried to cover it up."

The dichotomy between the Washington political mentality and the thinking of Americans living beyond the Potomac became more evident as Clinton's private life became weaponized for partisan advantage. Scandalous—and even illegal—as the actions might have been, nearly three-quarters of the citizenry were willing to separate sexual immorality (and attempts to keep it secret) from the public business of the presidency. In their collective judgment, what Clinton had done didn't rise to the level of a firing offense. The reaction to the impeachment imbroglio, which many observers interpreted as Republican revenge over the Democrats' treatment of Nixon back in 1973 and 1974, showed the distance between so many professional politicians stressing ideological partisanship and a huge percentage of voters for whom commonsensical pragmatism served as a more significant principle. That nexus, of course, is tricky territory to explore because pols and people often appear to come from different planets.

Exactly twenty years after the attacks on Bork and Wright, journalist Ronald Brownstein published a serious study about the state of American politics early in the twenty-first century. The title of the nearly five-hundred-page book describes his subject and captures the time with warning-flag words precisely arranged—*The Second Civil War: How Extreme Partisanship Has Paralyzed Washington and Polarized America*. In a series of punchy sentences staking out this contemporary battlefield, Brownstein writes, "The center in American politics is eroding. Confrontation is rising. The parties are separating. And the conflict between them is widening" (26).

Granted, vigorous partisanship is fundamental to any vibrant democracy, and the competition between programmatic proposals provides needed calisthenics for sound civic action. But partisanship becomes unhealthy and destructive when politicians play only among themselves, on their own teams, instead of participating with those on the other side. Intense partisanship escalates to hold-your-ground-at-any-cost polarization, making compromise less of an operating principle and more of a suspect maneuver. With the parties firmly planted on opposite sides of the political spectrum, the center becomes a barren, no-person's-land—and problems fester without getting resolved. Citizens outside the District of Columbia's beltway watch the Democratic and Republican versions of what resemble "extreme sports" for officeholders, becoming angry and frustrated at behavior they perceive as more childish than cooperative. In this environment, a president pays a high price with the public, including high-decibel charges of guilt through association.

A considerable degree of Barack Obama's original appeal as a new political face came from his keynote speech at the 2004 Democratic National Convention in Boston. At the time, he was a relatively unknown state senator from Illinois, who was running for a US Senate seat. Near the end of the address, Obama said,

> Even as we speak, there are those who are preparing to divide us, the spin masters and negative ad peddlers who embrace the politics of anything goes. Well, I say to them tonight there's not a liberal America and a conservative America; there's the United States of America. There's not a black America and white America and Latino America and Asian America; there's the United States of America. The pundits like to slice and dice our country into red states and blue states, red states for Republicans, blue states for Democrats. But I've got news for them, too. We worship an awesome God in the blue states, and we don't like federal agents poking around our libraries in the red states. We are one people, all of us pledging allegiance to the stars and stripes, all of us defending the United States of America.

Obama's remarks were more than a call for unity. They shrewdly identified how professional politicians and the media divided people into partisan camps—at the expense of national solidarity. As with the public's response to Clinton's impeachment, the willingness of Democrats, independents, and even some Republicans to cheer what Obama said exposed the problems of overly emphasizing a party line—or party color—to the exclusion of other relevant concerns. By introducing himself in this way, Obama was successful in positioning himself as different from other Democrats competing for national attention before the 2008 presidential campaign. Interestingly, eight years later, when Donald Trump ran for the White House on the Republican ticket, he also played down purely party concerns. The main thrust of his campaign to "Make America Great Again" was largely aimed at disrupting the status quo of Washington—of "draining the swamp" (in his phrase) of all the lobbyist money influencing legislation and of reducing the partisan feuding that was standing in the way of long-delayed priorities, including infrastructure projects. The real estate developer and reality-television performer projected himself to potential voters as the consummate dealmaker, a figure who could bring proponents of different viewpoints into a room to resolve differences—and solve problems.

With both Obama and Trump, initial impressions that they'd be willing to work across the Democratic-Republican divide proved to be wishful thinking rather than political reality. Once they were inaugurated, both Obama and Trump abandoned talk, let alone action, to promote cross-party comity and activity. In Obama's case, he learned early on (and one assumes to his considerable regret) that Republicans had one principal objective after he moved into the White House in early 2009. His desire for bipartisanship crashed into the political intransigence that's become a constant of Washington governmental practice. Before the 2010 midterm elections, Mitch McConnell, who was the Republican Senate minority leader, said, "The single most important thing we want to achieve is for President Obama to be a one-term president." For McConnell, his "single most important thing" wasn't winning majorities in Congress or passing legislation to benefit the citizenry of his country. McConnell failed in his goal of defeating Obama in 2012, but his remark serves as a salient reminder that partisan competition trumps any semblance of governmental cooperation in the current political environment. McConnell became Senate majority leader after the Republicans' success in the 2014 midterm elections. The current Senate minority leader is Chuck Schumer. Even before Trump was sworn into office in 2017, the president-elect was tweeting that Schumer was "head clown" of the Democrats in the Senate, the first of many disparaging comments directed at Trump's fellow New Yorker. At this time, bipartisan cooperation in Washington has all the vitality of a stuffed dodo bird.

The rise of partisanship, especially during recent years, has brought to the fore the primacy of a party's *base* at election time and in providing continuous support outside the voting booth. In the 2008 edition of *Safire's Political Dictionary*, the late *New York Times* columnist and Nixon speechwriter William Safire added the word *base*, defining it as "loyal constituencies that are considered to be a party's core of support." Explaining the term, which seems almost unavoidable in today's political discourse and journalism, he noted that during "the last half of the twentieth century, the idea of the fundament of support was called the power base; by the turn of the twenty-first, the noun could stand by itself, often attached to the verb *energize*" (44).

Emphasizing, exploiting, or energizing a party's base by digging more deeply into it comes at the expense of expanding political support to encompass more moderate independents or those who are inclined but not fully committed to one or the other party. At the end of every NBC News/*Wall Street Journal* survey, researchers ask respondents to identify themselves politically by using the following distinct categories:

Strong Democrat
Not very strong Democrat
Independent/lean Democrat
Strictly Independent
Independent/lean Republican
Not very strong Republican
Strong Republican
Other
Not sure

Invariably, fewer than a quarter of the people say they are either "Strong Democrat" or "Strong Republican," the most devout stalwarts in the base of each party. The largest percentage usually comes from adding together "Independent/lean Democrat," "Strictly Independent," and "Independent/lean Republican." Independents, however, can shift allegiances from election to election and lack the slam dunk reliability of straight-ticket voters.

Targeting the most loyal for attention, rather than adopting a broader approach, which is easier to do now with computer analysis of voter data, increases partisanship, causes a decline in moderate voters, and creates greater polarization on both the left and the right. On each of the extremes, political behavior seems a mirror image of itself, with similarities overwhelming differences.

Since the 1990s, the most conspicuous and consequential phenomenon in American politics has been the rise of what's called "negative partisanship" within the electorate. Gone are the times when a high percentage of voters looked up to the candidates and the party they favored and followed on the basis of their own merits, as opposed to reacting against the other party's candidates. Now, quite the opposite is taking place with greater frequency—and intensity. Citizens regard the opposing party and its figures with hostility bordering on hatred. Democrats see Republicans and Republicans view Democrats as objectionable, malignant, and worse. The negative charge, if you will, has become as strong—or, in most cases, stronger—as the positive one, shaping a new political environment with more antipathy and incompatibility. Divisions have deepened and taken on a surly, snarling tone. Voting *against* a candidate has become as common—or even more prevalent—than voting *for* someone.

This political animus is ascendant for self-identified members of both major parties. A Pew Research Center study in 2016 found that 21 percent of Republicans surveyed in 1994 had a "very unfavorable" opinion of the Democratic Party. That number jumped to 32 percent in 2008 and spiked to 58 percent in 2016. Responses of Democrats were almost identical. Their "very unfavorable" view of the GOP stood at 17 percent in 1994, at 37 percent in 2008, and at 55 percent in 2016. In the "unfavorable" category in 2016, 91 percent of Republicans saw the Democratic Party with a curled lip, while 86 percent of Democrats returned their lack of regard to the Republican Party. To be sure, negative advertising during campaigns and stridently partisan media outlets day in and day out exacerbate this negative partisanship. Writing in *Politico* a year after the 2016 election, political scientists Alan Abramowitz and Steven Webster used a vivid analogy to explain the current situation:

> Over the past few decades, American politics has become like a bitter sports rivalry, in which the parties hang together mainly out of sheer hatred of the other team, rather than a shared sense of purpose. Republicans might not love the president [Donald Trump], but they absolutely loathe his Democratic adversaries. And it's also true of Democrats, who might be consumed by their internal feuds over foreign policy and the proper role of government were it not for Trump. Negative partisanship explains nearly everything in American politics today—from why Trump's base is unlikely to abandon him even if, as he once said, he were to shoot someone on Fifth Avenue, to why it was so easy for vulnerable red-state Democrats to resist defecting on the health care bill.

Donald Trump's penchant for strenuously attacking perceived opponents in the Democratic Party conforms to this political moment almost perfectly, and his personality is in sync with the times. His demeaning nicknames for his opponents and his unrelenting put-downs strengthen his standing among his supporters. A question, however, arises concerning how far anyone's political backing might extend. During the 2018 midterm election season, Trump participated in nearly fifty rallies in states with competitive Senate, House, and gubernatorial contests. Ed Pilkington of the British newspaper the *Guardian* covered five such partisan gatherings during an eight-day period right before Election Day. Pilkington's reportage includes this rather chilling exchange with one attendee in Wisconsin:

> I ask him who he regards as his political enemies, and whether "hate" is too strong a word. "Not at all," he says.

"I have a deep and absolute disgust for these human beings."
Which ones? He rattles off CNN, [George] Soros, [Hillary]
Clinton, [Maxine] Waters, [Cory] Booker, "Pocahontas"
AKA Elizabeth Warren, and others. Why do you hate them?
"They want to turn America into a socialistic country. It's
disgusting." I ask [him] how far he is prepared to take his
hatred. In reply, he tells a story. The other day he talked to
his sister, who is liberal and votes Democratic. He said to
her: "If there is a civil war in this country and you were on
the wrong side, I would have no problem shooting you in
the face." You must be joking, I say. "No I am not. I love my
sister, we get on great. But she has to know how passionate
I am about our president."

Talk of politically motivated sororicide might seem like far-
fetched dialogue from a forgettable film with a sanguinary ex-
cess of violence. However, genuine fear related to the current
civic climate exists among the electorate. In the NPR/PBS News-
Hour/Marist National Poll conducted right before the 2018
midterm voting, the following question was posed: "How concerned are you that the negative tone and lack of civility in
Washington will lead to violence or acts of terror: Very concerned, concerned, not very concerned, or not concerned at all?"
Some 79 percent of respondents expressed that they were "very
concerned" or "concerned." Among likely voters, that percentage increased to 82 percent—but efforts to encourage civility
among officeholders and the media have thus far been roundly
ignored.

Interestingly, at the same time negative partisanship was
becoming influential in American political behavior, another
ballot-determining activity was developing within the electorate.
Straight-ticket voting, with its purposeful support of one party
to the exclusion of the other, has assumed an importance, indeed dominance, not registered in the past century. Results in
2016 illustrate the fact that casting a so-called split ticket is per-
ceptibly rare. During that presidential year, a total of thirty-four

Senate seats were also being contested nationally. In every one of those thirty-four states, the winner of the presidential race and the Senate victor represented the same party. Voters no longer choose person over party in the open-minded, American way you used to hear about in high school civics classes. Back in 1972, for example, 30 percent of the electorate supported either Richard Nixon or George McGovern *and* the congressional candidate of the opposing party. No more.

Taken together, negative partisanship and straight-ticket voting contribute to a laser-focused emphasis on the party's loyal, unwavering base of support, especially by aspirants and occupants of the White House. However, amid this new semantics of US politics, all the talk of "the base" as a noun also brings to mind the adjectival meaning of the word: inferior, unrefined, debased—as in the phrase "base currency." Lost in all of the attention to "the base" is a larger view of democracy and a broader concern for the common good that looks beyond the November ballot box to months and years of interest or involvement in public service.

However, as long as base-voting produces electoral victories—as it has most recently for Bush, Obama, and Trump—we'll continue to see the practice. Less-partisan citizens will loudly complain, but Washington won't really be listening. The ABC News Sunday program *This Week* aired the comments reproduced below during the summer of 2017, as Congress debated new health-care legislation. Martha Raddatz, the anchor of that week's show, interviewed several people in Ohio to gauge their reaction to what they saw unfolding on Capitol Hill:

RADDATZ: Everyone we talked to in Ohio, everyone, is concerned that putting country first is being lost, swallowed up in all the DC partisanship.
UNIDENTIFIED FEMALE. I really dislike the fact that it has to be one party against another. It doesn't seem like we're working together.

UNIDENTIFIED MALE. It appears to me that anybody that we elect doesn't seem to be working for us, they seem to be working for the party. It's either Democrat or it's Republican. It's not about the United States; it's about Democrats or Republicans. Who is against something? They're either all for or all against. That's all politics. It has nothing to do with our agenda.

UNIDENTIFIED MALE. Hopefully we can get a few people talking to each other instead of just arguing all the time.

UNIDENTIFIED FEMALE. I'm hoping that this will bring Congress together and get rid of some of this partisanship and have them actually take a look at these things without thinking about the next election. And do the job they're supposed to be doing. That's what I'd like to see.

The attitude that working together in a spirit of bipartisanship yields enlightened public policy is probably more romantic than realistic—a by-product of theoretical textbooks in political science, rather than actual governmental practices. More troubling, perhaps, is the growing animosity of party members that is directed at those of the opposite party. The political is becoming personal in basic impressions of other people. Five months before the 2016 election, the Pew Research Center released a detailed study that charted what Democrats thought of Republicans and vice versa. The percentage of Democrats who said Republicans were more close-minded than other Americans was more than two-thirds—70 percent. Just over half of the Republicans—52 percent—thought Democrats were close-minded. But those same Republicans said Democrats were more immoral (47 percent), more lazy (46 percent), and more dishonest (45 percent) than other Americans. Democrats saw Republicans as more dishonest (42 percent), more immoral (35 percent), and more unintelligent (33 percent). Taken together, these viewpoints indicate that the regard for the humanity of someone supporting the other political party is less suspicious than antipathetic.

Political divisions affect how we form opinions about people we know at work, at school, or in the neighborhood. One eye-opening survey (conducted in 2010 by the polling firm YouGov) found that 49 percent of Republicans and 33 percent of Democrats would be "displeased" if a child of theirs married someone in the opposite party. In 1960, the percentages were just 5 and 4, respectively, for Republicans and Democrats. A more recent study by Professor Lynn Vavreck at UCLA, published in the *New York Times* on January 31, 2017, included these findings: "In 1958, 33 percent of Democrats wanted their daughters to marry a Democrat, and 25 percent of Republicans wanted their daughters to marry a Republican. But by 2016, 60 percent of Democrats and 63 percent of Republicans felt that way." What Americans think about politics and where they direct their support are radically changing contemporary reactions to other people to degrees we haven't seen since opinion surveys became a principal tool for learning about other people and their viewpoints.

When political opinions of whatever mentality influence personal responses to nonpolitical subjects and situations, tribalism or something akin to it develops—and flourishes. Moreover, divisions become more pronounced, and daily friction sparks conflict through either words or actions. Assessing the political landscape before Election Day in an August 31, 2016, *New York Times* column, Thomas L. Friedman wrote, "Yes, I know, politics ain't bean bag. It's about winning. But it's also about winning with a mandate to govern. And right now everything suggests that the next four years will be just like the last eight: a gridlocked, toxic, Sunni-Shiite, Democrat-Republican civil war, with little search for common ground. That's how you ruin, not run, a great country."

So far Trump's presidency has continued the "Democrat-Republican civil war," and a multitude of White House actions have reversed Obama-era executive orders. When Republicans won the House majority in 2010—followed by the GOP gaining Senate control after the 2014 midterm elections—Obama could no longer push an agenda legislatively, so he established commissions, enacted regulations, and issued operating procedures by signing executive orders or presidential memoranda. Although these actions were binding during his time in office, his successor could—and often did—execute new orders to stop or to modify the provisions of the previous actions. Changing such legislation as, say, the Affordable Care Act, has proved to be much more difficult. Eisenhower kept the programs of FDR's New Deal functioning, and Nixon had other concerns than undoing the work of LBJ's Great Society. But overturning executive orders is as easy as signing a piece of paper, an act Trump has ceremoniously and proudly conducted in front of television cameras with a showman's gusto. What's lacking, of course, in this environment of political civil war is any sense of continuity in policy. Partisanship dictates the pendulum swing of the presidential pen.

Research in public opinion is telling in charting the extent to which the rise of partisanship has contributed to the polarization affecting incumbent presidents since the 1950s and early 1960s. According to data provided by the Pew Research Center, 49 percent of Democrats approved of Eisenhower, and the same percentage of Republicans approved of Kennedy. In each case, almost half the members of the opposing party held a positive view of the White House occupant. During the 1980s, Reagan enjoyed an average of 31 percent approval by Democrats for his performance in office.

In the 1990s, a starker decline began with Clinton, who received an average of 27 percent GOP approval. More recently, with partisanship becoming much stronger and negativity at whoever sits in the Oval Office increasingly fierce, the gap in approval that exists between members of the two parties is closer to an abyss. Just 14 percent of Republicans looked favorably on Obama, and that percentage sank to 7 percent of Democrats approving Trump after his first two years in office. These numbers—with the opinions and emotions they represent—show how divided America is politically and how difficult national unity is to achieve in this climate.

The US political system as constituted makes it impossible to remove partisan allegiances from the conduct of elections and government. It becomes a matter of degree, and of late seeking consensus or a shared sense of the common good seems less appealing to political professionals than accentuating partisanship above all. This situation makes legislating and the working relationship between Congress and the White House a continuing stress test. Robert Costa, a national political reporter for the *Washington Post* and the moderator of *Washington Week* on PBS, received access to a videotape showing former House Speaker John Boehner talking to a business group in Las Vegas in the summer of 2017. In Costa's July 25, 2017, account, Boehner told his audience "that cutting bipartisan deals in Washington is now all but impossible due to the way negotiations unfold in the media. Any interaction with a Democrat risks being covered by conservative outlets as a potential betrayal of the GOP, he said."

In this hyperpartisan environment, Boehner admitted that he would meet with President Barack Obama at the White House in secret. "If I didn't sneak in, if I went in like I would normally go in, the right-wing press would go crazy," he explained. "'What is Boehner up to?' The left-wing press would go just as crazy. 'What is Obama doing? He's going to let Boehner roll him again.' You're dead before you even have an agreement."

The same day Costa's article about Boehner appeared in the *Washington Post*, John McCain spoke on the floor of the Senate after being diagnosed with brain cancer. The remarks of the six-term senator from Arizona and 2008 Republican presidential candidate, who died on August 25, 2018, seemed nostalgic and valedictory—a veteran's summation and petition. Noting that the chamber's deliberations "are more partisan, more tribal more of the time than any other time I remember," McCain, a political realist, acknowledged "compromises that each side criticize but also accept" are necessary for the slow-moving machinery of government.

Addressing his colleagues directly, he took aim at the now-reigning, partisan proposition that victory at any cost should be the goal when resolving contending legislative viewpoints. "Our system doesn't depend on our nobility," he argued. "It accounts for our imperfections, and gives an order to our individual strivings that has helped make ours the most powerful and prosperous society on earth. It is our responsibility to preserve that, even when it requires us to do something less satisfying than 'winning.' Even when we must give a little to get a little. Even when our efforts manage just three yards and a cloud of dust, while critics on both sides denounce us for timidity, for our failure to 'triumph.'" Like Boehner, McCain connected the contemporary media—subject of the next chapter—to the sulfurous climate now dividing the parties. "I hope we can again rely on humility, on our need to cooperate, on our dependence on each other to learn how to trust each other again and by so doing better serve the people who elected us," he said. "Stop listening to the bombastic loudmouths on the radio and television and the Internet. To hell with them. They don't want anything done for the public good. Our incapacity is their livelihood."

In recent years, the consequences of what Boehner and McCain described are easy to see, especially from the vantage point of 1600 Pennsylvania Avenue by presidents, who might be inclined to negotiate compromises on difficult matters. As a result, institutionally, there's more gridlock, stalemate, and paralysis; individually, there's less comity, civility, and camaraderie. When such words as *cooperation, compromise,* and *consensus* become invectives in the American political dialect, polarization makes members of the two parties much less collegial and much more combative. As long as Democrats and Republicans continue to cater what they do to their bases, America can expect base politics and the polarized tribalism that such base politics produces and promotes.

FOUR

Conundrums of Communications

If American politics began to turn more ferociously partisan in 1987, the center-clearing polarization that resulted received rocketlike propulsion in the 1990s from the explosion of new media technologies. The multiplication of communication sources—particularly on the internet and via cable or satellite television—expanded the people's choices in selecting messages. This bounty, however, also brought mutiny. Traditional publications and programs lost audience, and pools of common, shared information started to contract to an alarming degree. Politically, communities of like-minded citizens sprang up on the left and right, making presidential governance and leadership different from the past—and much more difficult.

The communications environment has changed so dramatically since the 1990s that observers struggle to explain what's happened and the consequences for the US democratic system. Veteran television correspondent Tom Brokaw suggested that "we are in the middle of another Big Bang." Commenting in *No Time to Think: The Menace of Speed and the 24-Hour News Cycle* (2008), Brokaw went on to say, "We've created this universe in which all these planets are suddenly out there colliding with each other. We are trying to determine which ones will support life, which ones will drift too close to the sun and burn up, which ones will meld with another. And the effect of it all is bewildering, both to those of us in this end of the spectrum [the media providers] and those who are on the receiving end [the audience]. It's a big dilemma and we haven't given enough thought to the consequences" (12).

From a political perspective, a planetary guide to informational outlets of this Big Bang would include everything from the White House website (Bill Clinton's administration inaugurated the first one in 1994) to partisan-oriented television channels (the Fox News channel and MSNBC both began airing in 1996) to ideological news and opinion aggregators (the Drudge Report became available on the internet in 1997). Since the 1990s, Facebook (begun in 2004), YouTube (started in 2005), Twitter (launched in 2006), and many other cyber-based outlets have delivered political messages of one kind or another in ways that are not only (to use Brokaw's word) "bewildering" but also beguiling in the sense of appealing to established political viewpoints. Today's media landscape, unlike the earlier and earthbound one without colliding asteroids to worry about, makes it much easier to receive just the news, analysis, and commentary you desire, and which conforms to—and often repeatedly confirms—what you already think about an issue or public figure.

In the past, relatively few sources (popularly called "the mass media") competed for attention. Certain slants and biases were noticeable—for example, an attraction to "the new," to change, to conflict, to negative information—but overt and consistent political side-taking was rare in mainstream outlets. To cater to a wide, diverse audience, major publications and broadcast entities tended to steer their content to the middle of the road. When there were only three commercial television networks, four or five truly national newspapers, and a handful of respectable magazines, there was an emphasis on reporting what was happening rather than pushing a partisan or personal viewpoint. Facts were supreme.

To show what the development of new communication forms has meant to evening network news alone, a comparison of the past to the present is revealing. In 1980, the year CNN started, 52 million people (out of nearly 227 million Americans) watched the dinnertime newscasts on ABC, CBS, and NBC. That meant 75 percent of TV sets in the United States were tuned in to network news. According to data from the Nielsen Company, the total viewership for the evening news on ABC, CBS, and NBC for the 2017–18 season was just below 23 million—far less than half the 1980 audience—at a time when the US population exceeds 325 million. Is it any wonder why we now see less international news—which is quite expensive—on network broadcasts? Shorter sound bites, too, make sure viewers won't become bored when a complex political subject receives attention. In newspapers and magazines, the injection of "attitude," cutting or critical statements embedded in a news story, is intended to keep a reader from turning to another article or publication.

For a president, the new media ecosystem means developing original or novel communication practices that adapt to the array of evolving technologies. The concept of "broadcasting," by and large, still applies to the networks, but it's more appropriate to think in terms of "narrowcasting" for cable or satellite distribution, and even "slivercasting" applies in the case of web-based visual or audio features that are now often offered independently or in addition to regular programs. Written words still arrive printed on paper, but websites, blogs, and social media provide an endless flow of additional, frequently opinion-laden, statements of political content. Moreover, the romance between journalism and entertainment has developed into a long-term affair that has resulted in presidents or aspirants to the office making their way to comedy programs with increasing frequency. The stagecraft of statecraft has expanded well beyond Theodore Roosevelt's "bully pulpit," as technological innovations and programming developments have multiplied the ways political messages are delivered in the twenty-first century.

The wealth of sources produces so much "content" that a citizen can either rely on familiar, trusted outlets or take the initiative to seek out a variety of reports or interpretations addressing a particular subject. To be sure, it's easier (and less time-consuming) to turn to a publication, program, or website someone already knows. In today's environment, however, a dependence on certain sources can result in receiving information and opinion with which a person already agrees. This can lead to reinforcement of one viewpoint, rather than the exploration of competing or conflicting ones—and, therefore, contribute to more and more polarization. All the talk of "information silos," with their restricted vision beyond one perspective, can encourage someone to worry about "information ghettos" and everything that ugly phrase might imply.

In a column published shortly after Barack Obama's election in 2008, Michael Gerson, who served as George W. Bush's chief speechwriter before becoming a columnist for the *Washington Post*, surveyed the communications landscape of that campaign and shrewdly observed, "Because of the ideological polarization of cable television news, talk radio and the Internet, Americans can now get their information from entirely partisan sources. They can live, if they choose to, in an ideological world of their own creation, viewing anyone outside that world as an idiot or criminal, and finding many who will cheer their intemperance." That's the way we were a decade or so ago.

In the years since 2008, the situation has become even more acute. A survey by Gallup in 2016 found that just 32 percent of Americans trusted the mass media—the lowest level ever in

Gallup's polling and down from 43 percent eight years earlier. Among Republicans, only 14 percent reported trusting the mass media, a decline from 32 percent the year before. A political figure, such as Donald Trump, can take advantage of this perception by railing against the "fake news" of the mainstream media, but it also means a sizable number of citizens will search for sources in which they do have confidence, if they are inclined to pursue the background of political topics. Should this mean going to outlets with an established partisan orientation, divisions can deepen and make consensus unlikely. A vicious cycle quickly becomes a downward spiral, transporting someone away from an open-minded search for the merits, pro and con, of a complex governmental proposal.

The new media technologies dramatically changed the relationship between a citizen and the panoply of political communication. They also created additional and unending demands for a president in governing and leading. Adapting to this environment requires an understanding of what's possible, why it's important, and how best to deliver messages that accomplish their purpose. Back in the 1960s, when he was president of France, Charles de Gaulle asked an aide, "How can you be expected to govern a country that has 246 different kinds of cheese?" Nowadays a leader's exasperation might be more specifically directed at the vast smorgasbord of information sources and figuring out the most useful strategy for dealing with the media in their diverse multiplicity. (The word *media*, which is the correct Latin plural of "medium," should grammatically take a plural verb—despite the repeatedly incorrect contemporary usage that implies a collectivity of information outlets working together that doesn't exist. In most situations, competition drives the performance of one medium against other media.)

During his presidency, Ronald Reagan was often referred to as "the great communicator" for his speaking and speechmaking prowess on television. His staff also made sure to provide him with what was then called "the line of the day," a scripted, specific message that microphones and cameras captured to emphasize a policy or proposal the administration wanted the public to know about. The strategy was successful for Reagan for the simple reason that it conformed to the time. The growth in new technologies was just beginning. (In 1980, there were just twenty-eight cable TV networks. By 1990, the number had spiked to seventy-nine—and the World Wide Web was starting to come online, with 130 websites available by 1993.)

As mentioned earlier, the 1990s were a critically significant decade in the history of the media. Indeed, a Rubicon (of sorts) was crossed in presidential communication on April 19, 1994, when a young woman got up on MTV and asked Bill Clinton, "Mr. President, the world's dying to know, is it boxers or briefs?" The discussion program *Enough Is Enough* focused on violence in America and proved revealing beyond the inquiry about the leader of the free world's underwear. With the burgeoning galaxy of media outlets, a president (and his staff) could no longer count on the major broadcast networks to reach the entire spectrum of voters with any "line of the day." In this circumstance, younger citizens were more likely to be watching music videos than news programs, so Clinton appeared where this constituency would be more liable to see him.

Since the 1990s—which seem like a much simpler time and very long ago—targeting messages for specific age, gender, or racial background during campaigns has become increasingly sophisticated for both informational statements and for paid advertisements. For example, during his White House days, George W. Bush's popping up on ESPN to chat about baseball was part of an overall strategy of staying connected with potentially friendly voters—and sports fans. Especially in his second term, Barack Obama appeared in a variety of nontraditional settings, including the absurdist-interview series *Between Two Ferns* on the video website Funny or Die. That program, which aired in 2014, drew over twenty-eight million views, most of them (like Clinton's MTV audience) by young people.

Almost a year later, Obama granted interviews to *Vox* and *BuzzFeed*, two news sites offering strong connections to millennials, in an effort to enlarge a president's megaphone to include new media "platforms." *BuzzFeed* also produced a two-minute video of Obama taking selfies and kidding around in front of a camera. That production drew some fifty million views, while the State of the Union Address a couple weeks earlier was watched by 31.7 million people on the thirteen different television networks that carried the speech, according to Nielsen's count. A short video of offbeat humor that goes viral will trump a serious discussion of policy any time; however, in this particular case, the audience for the levity on a media venue that began to cover more serious news in late 2011 is nearly double in size.

During Obama's interview with *Vox*, which launched in 2014, he spoke directly about contemporary media and their relationship to the increase in today's political polarization. The president complained that "the balkanization of the media means that we just don't have a common place where we get common facts and a common worldview the way we did 20, 30 years ago. And that just keeps on accelerating, you know. And I'm not the first to observe this, but you've got the Fox News/ Rush Limbaugh folks and then you've got the MSNBC folks. . . . But the point is that technology which brings the world to us allows us to narrow our point of view."

Obama's emphasis on the absence of "a common place," "common facts," and "a common worldview," a theme to which he still frequently returns in his public appearances since leaving office, illustrates the extent to which people of differing opinions can inhabit alternate realities on the basis of journalistic reports shaped by information with a definite political bias. The first chapter of *Public Opinion* (1922), Walter Lippmann's seminal interpretation of news, is called "The World Outside and the Pictures in Our Heads." The pictures of the world we carry around will be dissimilar and not really comparable if their origins and motivations start at entirely different points.

The shift from "common" to "narrow" encompasses much more than what a person might know or imagine.

Although Obama mentioned gerrymandering and campaign spending as contributing to greater polarization, he returned in his interview with *Vox* to the impact of the media and offered advice to his White House successor: "People are absorbing an entirely different reality when it comes to politics, even though the way they're living their lives and interacting with each other isn't that polarizing. So my advice to a future president is increasingly try to bypass the traditional venues that create divisions and try to find new venues within this new media that are quirkier, less predictable."

Vox interviewed Obama on February 9, 2015, about six months before Donald J. Trump announced his candidacy for president. There's no way the forty-fourth president could have been thinking of his successor's "quirkier, less predictable" use of new media, such as Twitter, Facebook and YouTube; however, during his campaign and subsequently, Trump has relied on social media to build and sustain his connections to his core supporters and to others, a situation discussed in detail later in this book. Since June 16, 2015, when Trump told the world he would seek the White House, journalists and political observers have closely followed Trump's tweets to gauge his thinking, to monitor his level of outrage, and to receive a sense of his upcoming decisions and actions.

America has never had a president like Trump—a chief executive and commander in chief who has neither had day-to-day involvement in government nor served in the military. However, his background in traditional media (fourteen seasons of prime-time television, several best-selling books, and countless other television and radio appearances) and his insatiable need for social media activity provide a foundation for the public dimensions of serving as president. He is intimately aware of what it means to be a celebrity and the center of attention.

However, a considerable irony of Trump's political success coming from his daily involvement with multiple forms of communication and his unrelenting use of those messages to wage war against what he considers a (if not *the*) principal adversary—the media. Unfailingly, biographical studies of past presidents going back to the Virginia dynasty include fulminations against press coverage. Reporters don't know the whole story, a figure will charge, and then storm that a portrayal of a policy or action is unfair or incomplete. Near the end of his presidency, Jefferson thundered in a letter, "I really look with commiseration over the great body of my fellow citizens, who, reading newspapers, live & die in the belief, that they have known something of what has been passing in the world in their time." A democratic republic breeds such carping criticism, and it often takes place in private, within the walls of the White House or in epistles to friends.

In *Report on the Virginia Resolutions,* James Madison, who succeeded Jefferson as president, composed a more measured and reality-based assessment of the press and its value, when he wrote:

> Some degree of abuse is inseparable from the proper use of every thing, and in no instance is this more true than in that of the press. It has accordingly been decided by the practice of the States, that it is better to leave a few of its noxious branches to their luxuriant growth, than, by pruning them away, to injure the vigour of those yielding the proper fruits. And can the wisdom of this policy be doubted by any who reflect that to the press alone, chequered as it is with abuses, the world is indebted for all the triumphs which have been gained by reason and humanity over error and oppression; who reflect that to the same beneficent source the United States owe much of the lights which conducted them to the ranks of a free and independent nation, and which have improved their political system into a shape so auspicious to their happiness?

Mature leaders understand that "noxious branches" will lead to political journalism "chequered as it with abuses"—but, on the whole, "the triumphs" and "much of the lights" are consequences of a free press and its imperfect work.

In public, until Trump took the oath of office, presidents would usually keep evaluations of journalism to themselves, make light of news treatment, or praise the role of a press protected by the First Amendment—or all three. For example, at a press conference on May 9, 1962, when John Kennedy was asked about "the treatment of your Administration, treatment of the issues of the day," the president, according to the transcript in the Kennedy Library, responded, "Well, I am reading more and enjoying it less—(laughter)—..., but I have not complained nor do I plan to make any general complaints. I read, and talk to myself about it, but I don't plan to issue any general statement of the press. I think they are doing their task, as a critical branch, the fourth estate, and I am attempting to do mine, and we are going to live together for a period, and then go our separate ways (more laughter)." Six months later during a television interview, Kennedy returned to the complex, negative-positive relationship between the president and the press: "It is never pleasant to be reading things that are not agreeable news," he observed, "but I would say that it is an invaluable arm of the presidency, as a check really on what is going on in the administration, and more things come to my attention that cause me concern or give me information. . . . Even though we never like it, and even though we wish they didn't write it, and even though we disapprove, there isn't any doubt that we could not do the job at all in a free society without a very, very active press." As many "even though" clauses as he deploys to register a newsmaker's reservations, JFK understood the vital function of the media in a democracy. With the exception of Richard Nixon, who was hostile to journalists and treated them as unredeemable opponents, Kennedy's successors have, by and large, tolerated the media's coverage and kept their criticism either muted or targeted to specific stories.

Trump's approach is Nixonianism performing on the most potent growth hormone, with an anabolic steroid chaser as a kicker for good measure. Throughout the 2016 campaign and ever since Election Day, Trump has treated the news media as an ongoing opponent and object of ridicule. During rallies, he has no reluctance to single out journalists, belittling them in front of crowds and creating tension between the candidate's supporters and what he has called "those sleazebags" and "scum" assigned to cover them. Since fall 2016, some news executives have seriously worried that violence might be directed at their reporters. Critical as Trump was as a candidate, he has been even more aggressive and combative in confronting the media since winning the White House, with Twitter his cyber cudgel.

In December 2016, Trump began tweeting tirades and making public statements that accused mainstream journalistic outlets of being—in his signature phrase—"FAKE NEWS." One tweet, which launched thousands of words of commentary, appeared on February 17, 2017: "The FAKE NEWS media (failing @nytimes, @NBCNews, @ABC, @CBS, @CNN) is not my enemy, it is the enemy of the American People!" By designating journalistic institutions as "the enemy of the American people," Trump (wittingly or not) was using an epithet with a history reaching back to the French Revolution and the Stalin era in the Soviet Union. It would be difficult to come up with a more malignant insult. Yet he did. On October 29, 2018, in the wake of the horrific mass shooting at a Pittsburgh synagogue that killed eleven worshippers, he again expressed his antipathy to the press on Twitter by partially blaming journalism for the tragedy. In a two-part tweet, he wrote, "There is great anger in our Country caused in part by inaccurate, and even fraudulent, reporting of the news. The Fake News Media, the true Enemy of the People, must stop the open & obvious hostility & report the news accurately & fairly. That will do much to put out the flame. . . of Anger and Outrage and we will then be able to bring all sides together in Peace and Harmony. Fake News Must End!" Adding the word "true" to the phrase "Enemy of the People" in the context of a heinous crime proved too much for many observers of American democracy, but their outcry did nothing to still the president's thumbs.

Trump's obsession with the news media and how they cover him seems juvenile—doesn't the nation's leader have more serious concerns to occupy his time?—but there's a definite purpose to it. By repeating the term "fake news" over and over, he delegitimizes the various sources of information providing reportage, analysis, and commentary focused on him and his administration. In a way, he is trying to inoculate himself as much as he can against the impact of negative stories. If he's even modestly successful in making people think criticism directed at him is dishonest, and indeed fraudulent, whatever might be revealed would be suspect or dismissed outright.

By calling Ted Cruz "Lyin' Ted," Marco Rubio "Little Marco," Jeb Bush "Low Energy Jeb," and Hillary Clinton "Crooked Hillary," Trump, a brand name he himself built for his far-flung business empire, shrewdly branded his 2016 political opponents with vivid, demeaning nicknames that defined them in the minds of many voters. The phrase "fake news" plays a similar role, though in this case Trump appropriated a designation, often originating overseas, for fabricated and false stories that appeared on websites and social media feeds during his own presidential campaign. Articles trumpeting that Pope Francis had endorsed Trump, that Hillary Clinton was involved in child-abuse activity at a Washington pizza parlor, and that the leader of ISIS told American Muslims to vote for Clinton circulated before Election Day were without an iota of truth. Despite factual explanations of unfactual messages of unknowable influence that widely appeared during the fall campaign in 2016, "fake news" became Trump's favorite trope to refer to the work of the mainstream news media. In his first year as president, he tweeted nearly two hundred times about "fake news," brandishing the phrase like a sword, as well as a shield. He continued this branding operation into 2018, with a similar number of blasts, and the phrase over time took on *his* meaning rather than the original one.

Trump went far beyond 140-typed characters in railing against journalism during public appearances after his inauguration. At one event in Florida on February 18, 2017, he told a rally that he wanted "to speak . . . without the filter of the fake news." He then proceeded to devote several sentences to his allegations and grievances in a chapter-and-verse denunciation. What he said became the template for his often-repeated indictment of press abuse and resentment later in his presidency:

> The dishonest media which has published one false story after another with no sources, even though they pretend they have them, they make them up in many cases, they just don't want to report the truth and they've been calling us wrong now for two years. They don't get it. But they're starting to get it. I can tell you that. They've become a big part of the problem. They are part of the corrupt system. Thomas Jefferson, Andrew Jackson, and Abraham Lincoln and many of our greatest presidents fought with the media and called them out often times on their lies. When the media lies to people, I will never, ever let them get away with it. I will do whatever I can that they don't get away with it. They have their own agenda and their agenda is not your agenda. In fact, Thomas Jefferson said, "nothing can be believed which is seen in a newspaper." "Truth itself," he said, "becomes suspicious by being put into that polluted vehicle," that was June 14, my birthday, 1807. But despite all their lies, misrepresentations, and false stories, they could not defeat us in the primaries, and they could not defeat us in the general election, and we will continue to expose them for what they are, and most importantly, we will continue to win, win, win. We are not going to let the fake news tell us what to do, how to live, or what to believe. We are free and independent people and we will make our own choices.

One consequence of Trump's continuing assault on the mainstream news media is that his supporters now flock to information outlets that treat him favorably—with a positive, boosterlike bias. When this happens, of course, partisanship, polarization, and tribalism increase, making any working together by Republicans and Democrats in Washington even more difficult. In effect, the wealth of communication sources that currently exists makes it possible for citizens of whatever viewpoint to make political decisions on the basis of realities (or medialities) they selected, if not created, on their own. The absence of an agreed-on set of facts as the starting point for intelligent debate between the different sides of a policy issue makes the resolution of a political or ideological argument increasingly unlikely, if not inconceivable.

Compounding the problem of "fake news," both real and imagined, is the growing worry that the disseminators have calculated reasons for circulating false information and hope to achieve a specific effect. Indeed, in 2016, *Oxford Dictionaries* named *post-truth* the international word of the year for its significance in that year's presidential campaign and in Great Britain's referendum about staying or leaving the European Union. In announcing the word's selection (or election), Oxford University Press defined *post-truth* as "relating to or devoting circumstances in which objective facts are less influential in shaping public opinion than appeals to emotion and personal belief." The April 3, 2017, issue of *Time* asked on its cover "Is Truth Dead?" and the June 2017 edition of *National Geographic* featured "Why We Lie" as its major cover story.

A maxim about journalism characterizes it as "the first rough draft of history," and implicit in the words *first, rough,* and *draft* is the possibility that what's being reported might be incomplete or even inaccurate. Further serious and methodical probing—what might qualify as "history"—promises future correction and clarification. That process, however, breaks down in a "post-truth" world or environment that depends more on emotions than provable facts. This new "reality" also defies a time-honored belief, dating back to John Milton's *Areopagitica* (1644), that "Truth" will overcome "Falsehood" when they compete "in a free and open encounter." In the American context, Supreme Court justice Oliver Wendell Holmes Jr. proposed a more contemporary metaphor in his dissent about *Abrams v. United States*, envisioning a marketplace of ideas. In his description, Holmes wrote:

> When men have realized that time has upset many fighting faiths, they may come to believe even more than they believe the very foundations of their own conduct that the ultimate good desired is better reached by free trade in ideas—that the best test of truth is the power of the thought to get itself accepted in the competition of the market, and that truth is the only ground upon which their wishes safely can be carried out. That, at any rate, is the theory of our Constitution. It is an experiment, as all life is an experiment. Every year, if not every day, we have to wager our salvation upon some prophecy based upon imperfect knowledge.

The "free trade in ideas" with its "competition of the market" will, over time, yield "truth" in Holmes's famous formulation, which appeared in 1919. A century later, the image of a marketplace or of a public square seems quaint or even anachronistic—linguistic throwbacks to less complicated times, when the value of truth seemed higher and worth the pursuit involved in a continuing test or experiment.

Today the marketplace has become so crowded with conflicting messages from innumerable sources that contested issues and certain facts never seem to get completely resolved. Truth itself strains to emerge if a public figure—say, a president—keeps uttering blatant falsehoods that supporters believe and don't want to challenge. In this media-rich milieu, consensus is almost impossible to achieve, and the so-called public square might more accurately be described as a sprawling city, with countless squares, circles, and triangles of contending information and viewpoints.

Access to the plethora of political platforms in the twenty-first century might appear to be a modern marvel, offering concerned citizens a choice of media they've never had before.

Informative, even instructive, as that can be, selecting the most appropriate messages that contribute to civic understanding involves an active, deliberate, and sustained process. Evaluating a variety of different sources and what they are saying takes time and personal initiative. Getting to the bottom of a political subject or studying a president's decision making has never been more possible. But separating truth from falsehood, substance from spin, activity from mere motion requires constant surveillance and appraisal of the media environment (or marketplace) to find credible, trustworthy information. One publication or channel or website is never enough. And media of a single ideological perspective reinforce but don't really enlighten.

Tim Russert, the former moderator of *Meet the Press* on NBC and a model political analyst for his fairness and impartiality in discussing presidents and political candidates, delivered a lecture at the University of Notre Dame not long before his untimely death in 2008. He explained his preparation for interviews, but what he said could serve as a valuable primer for any citizen trying to grapple with public questions and issues. "I read the *New York Times* and the *Washington Times*," he said. "I read *The New Republic* and *The National Review*. I read *The Nation* and *Human Events*. I read left, right, and center. Many of my friends say that I now have confused myself, and they might be right. But I think it is imperative for an independent journalist, someone who is trying to ascertain to the very best of his or her ability what is the truth of the candidates' positions. What is their consistency? What is their intellectual grasp and understanding of the issues confronting us?"

Though his purpose was professional, Russert's approach reflects the obligation of citizenship—the responsibility of thought and action—we all share. Interestingly, from the other side of the press-politics relationship, if not divide, Obama voiced his concerns about the "24/7 echo chamber" of the media during a commencement address at the University of Michigan in 2010. His remedy to reduce political division and polarization sounded remarkably similar to Russert's:

If we choose to actively seek out information that challenges our assumptions and our beliefs, perhaps we can begin to understand where the people who disagree with us are coming from.

Now, this requires us to agree on a certain set of facts to debate from. That's why we need a vibrant and thriving news business that is separate from opinion makers and talking heads. That's why we need an educated citizenry that values hard evidence and not just assertion. As Senator Daniel Patrick Moynihan famously once said, "Everybody is entitled to his own opinion, but not his own facts."

Still, if you're somebody who only reads the editorial page of the *New York Times*, try glancing at the page of the *Wall Street Journal* once in a while. If you're a fan of Glenn Beck or Rush Limbaugh, try reading a few columns on the Huffington Post website. It may make your blood boil; your mind may not be changed. But the practice of listening to opposing views is essential for effective citizenship. It is essential for our democracy.

After leaving office, Obama continued to point out the potential civic problem that the contemporary news media climate presents. Speaking at Rice University's Baker Institute for Public Policy (named for former secretary of state and Republican Party stalwart James A. Baker) in late 2018, the former president compared the past with trusted television anchors to the current situation. "Whether it was [Walter] Cronkite or [David] Brinkley or what have you, there was a common set of facts, a baseline around which both parties had to adapt and respond to," Obama remarked. "By the time I take office, what you increasingly have is a media environment in which if you are a Fox News viewer, you have an entirely different reality than if you are a *New York Times* reader."

Citizens forming their opinions on entirely different realities create a divided nation politically, a situation Baker pointed out. "The responsible center in American politics has disappeared," he observed. "You have the advent of the internet, and that really makes it easy to be divisive. Divisiveness sells." Can people who are conditioned by differing realities constructed by competing facts—or highly suspicious information—ever come together and unite with a common purpose?

De Gaulle's worrisome question—"How can you be expected to govern a country that has 246 different kinds of cheese?"—remains enormously relevant for an American president in the twenty-first century if you think in terms of the more than 246 communication outlets, rather than of one specific type of food. Unifying the nation amid such informational choice is just one potential problem. In a post-truth time, a president needs to be even more careful in communicating with the public and have a consistent, cross-media strategy. Effective leadership and committed followership go hand in hand—but only if the leader and the citizens jointly make the effort, without any fakery on either side.

A well-functioning and self-governing nation depends on the examination and evaluation of credible information shared among its citizenry. Contemporary technologies make that kind of information instantly available, if we take the effort and make the time to find it. As the Constitutional Convention of 1787 ended, Benjamin Franklin was approached by a woman, who inquired, "Well, Doctor, what have we got, a republic or a monarchy?" Franklin quickly answered, "A republic, if you can keep it."

The American republic today is wired to a communications world that combines potential promise and dangerous peril. Resolving that continuing tension by constantly seeking the truth from many different sources will determine whether the president and the voters keep their republic during the twenty-first century.

—— FIVE ——

Reveries of Reform

Since two o'clock on the afternoon of April 30, 1789, when George Washington stood on the balcony of Federal Hall in New York City and took the oath as America's first president, each of his successors has fought the treacherous waves from the "ocean of difficulties"—Washington's phrase—that come with the office. The man who was "first in war, first in peace, and first in the hearts of his countrymen" understood that what he called, in an April 1789 letter to Henry Knox, "the chair of Government" would never have it easy, despite the sovereignlike trappings that a democratically elected leader might enjoy in republican service.

The tension between being simultaneously "one of us" *and* "one above others" has always tested US presidents, but that duality is ultimately of secondary consequence to the daily reality of making decisions about domestic issues or international affairs. Could changes to current laws, procedures, or practices strengthen the presidency and reduce some of the risks that await any occupant of the White House? Some proposals for reform could help alleviate recurring difficulties and ensure an institutional foundation that's sturdier and more secure.

The nominating process for presidential candidates is the first systemic activity that deserves examination and reconsideration. Back in 1968, fifteen states conducted primaries, and that year Hubert H. Humphrey, Lyndon Johnson's vice president, became the Democratic Party's standard-bearer without competing in a single contest, while two senators—Eugene McCarthy and Robert Kennedy—slugged it out all the way to early June in California, where Kennedy won and was assassinated. Elaine C. Kamarck describes the consequences of that fateful year in *Why Presidents Fail: And How They Can Succeed Again* (2016): "The turmoil from the Vietnam War, the civil rights movement, and the women's movement all collided at the 1968 Democratic convention and resulted in a demand that ordinary citizens have a say in the presidential nomination process. Since then, the system has moved from one in which politicians had a big voice and average voters had a very little voice to one in which voters have a very big voice and politicians a very little voice" (147).

The Democrats weren't alone. The Republican Party opened up its nominating procedures in the 1970s, and by 1976, both major parties were conducting primaries in twenty-eight states—nearly double the number from eight years earlier. In 2016, forty-one states held Democratic primaries, and thirty-nine held Republican ones. By that time, few members of either party could remember what it was like for in-the-know political elders to meet privately in smoke-filled rooms at state and national conventions to debate the pluses and minuses of prospective nominees.

The design of the American governmental system emphasizes balance, consistency, and deliberation. There is both coherence and rationality to the three independent branches of government (executive, legislative, and judicial), with their intertwining roles, that the framers of the Constitution created. In the frequently cited formulation of Richard E. Neustadt in *Presidential Power*, the federal government should be viewed as "separated institutions *sharing* powers" (33). Despite debates, disputes, and discord, especially between the White House and Capitol Hill, the arrangement of the process is understandable to anyone in a basic civics class.

Unfortunately, no civics teacher in America today could offer a clear or cogent explanation of the various procedures involved in the selection of candidates seeking the presidency— an office with, among other responsibilities, the duty of appointing federal judges, who serve until they resign, die, or are removed from the bench. The current selection system is hopelessly complex and convoluted to the point that average citizens can't easily comprehend the state-by-state competition that ultimately yields a major party's standard-bearer. The process itself, which seems mysterious and off-putting, results in increased clout for more extreme party activists in determining who emerges at the end of the gauntlet that's come into being over the past several decades. Theodore H. White, whose books on the presidential campaigns of 1960 through 1972 engagingly chronicle a bygone time, looked back on American elections from 1956 to 1980 in his 1982 volume, *America in Search of Itself*. Commenting on the 1980 nominating process, which involved thirty-six GOP primaries and thirty-one Democratic ones, White wrote, "There was no longer any way of making a simple generalization about how Americans chose their candidates for the presidency. What was worse, no school, no textbook, no course of instruction, could tell young Americans, who would soon be voting, how their system worked. And if we of the political press had to cram such rules into our heads as we moved from state to state, each with two parties, and each state differing—how could ordinary voters understand what professional observers had such difficulty grasping?" (289). White aptly summarized what he saw developing as "the madness of a good idea run wild." Making the process more democratically participatory had given individual states the power to play around with their rules and dates—with each quadrennial election cycle different from previous ones. But this meant that learning the ins-and-outs of the rules for a particular year had often become useless information by the next election cycle, as states schemed and jockeyed to exert additional clout on the selection system. In 2017, for example, California passed legislation to move the date of its 2020 primary from June to March 3, after the initial, seemingly sacred early competitions in Iowa, New Hampshire, Nevada, and South Carolina. To be near the head of the line, of course, means having more say, which is why the Golden State is not alone in wanting its primary exactly a month after the Iowa caucuses in 2020. Eight other contests—including those in Texas, North Carolina, Massachusetts, and Virginia—are already on that "Super Tuesday" schedule.

This every-state-for-itself attitude is ridiculous in a process that leads to the election of the country's national leader. Why should Iowa (with its caucus) or New Hampshire (with its primary) capture so much media attention and create the influence they do for the simple reason that they are the first political contests—and personal tests—of a lengthy ordeal? Is Iowa or New Hampshire representative of the Union demographically, economically, culturally, or in any other way? Who decreed that these two states—each over 90 percent white in demographic terms—would play such an outsized role in deciding the fate of candidates, especially whether pursuit of the nomination might remain feasible, should a candidate lose an early primary in one of these small states?

To show how ludicrous the situation can be, all you have to do is look back a few years. In 2012, Mitt Romney was proclaimed the victor of the Iowa caucuses the evening of balloting, receiving extensive coverage for his razor-thin, eight-vote margin. Sixteen days later, state GOP leaders reversed the results after a recount, declaring former Pennsylvania senator Rick Santorum the official winner by thirty-four votes. By that time, the New Hampshire primary had already taken place. Romney had triumphed there, and the media had reported his *second* electoral success, triggering wider positive coverage and its attendant momentum. What had actually happened in Iowa became a mere footnote to a future-oriented process when it became news days afterward. By then the political carnival had moved on.

Until 1845, the twenty-six states in the United States conducted their elections for president within a four- to five-week period during November and early December. Individual states set the exact day to go to the polls. An act of Congress, approved on January 23, 1845, formally established the Tuesday after the first Monday in November as the mandated "uniform time for holding elections for electors of President and Vice President in all the States of the Union." Congress should once again impose order on an important voting process, specifically the way candidates for the nation's highest office are chosen, by taking the patchwork-quilt approach out of the hands of the parties and the states. Legislation would remove the chaos and confusion that make an incomprehensible state-by-state electoral odyssey a problematic (at best) way of picking the major candidates for the fall campaign.

Ending once and for all any state's undeserved and privileged advantage has to be the objective of any initiative to reform the desperately broken method that keeps changing in haphazard fashion before each presidential election. A national primary, which would occur on a single day, really wouldn't allow enough time for aspirants to discuss their proposals for policies and ideas about presidential leadership. Voters without a doubt benefit from an extended appraisal of would-be nominees, whether from campaign appearances, speeches, or debates.

A regional primary system—say, five geographical regions with ten states in each region—would spread out the time for considering candidates and keep them campaigning in distinct yet contiguous areas of the country. The first region might go to the polls the first Tuesday of March, with each of the next four regions following successively in April, May, June, and July. Under this scheme, the primaries would end right around, for utilitarian and symbolic reasons, July 4th. The national conventions—to confirm each party's choice, to announce the vice-presidential running mate, and to adopt the party platform—could take place in late August or early September, reserving the weeks after Labor Day for coast-to-coast campaigning and debates.

Avoiding any regional favoritism is essential. That's why the order or sequence for voting should not be set until late January of the election year itself. One way to establish the progression from region to region would be for the incumbent president, who (one trusts) is concerned about the welfare of the institution and its future, to pick five slips of paper from a bowl held by the Speaker of the House of Representatives at the end of that year's State of the Union address. This act would undoubtedly be widely covered by the media, would link the executive and legislative branches, and would dramatize the importance of the national primary process, whose chief virtues would feature its emphasis on fairness, coherence, and impartiality. Each candidate could establish a distinct message before focusing on the first and subsequent regions. One ten-state group per month would be manageable because of the relative proximity of the states to one another. Moreover, the mixture of cities, suburbs, exurbs, and rural areas would force a candidate to develop a comprehensive, governing perspective not just for a particular region but also for the country as a whole.

To be sure, congressional action becomes complicated, even problematic, if senators or House members are themselves eyeing White House runs. Alienating the citizens of Iowa or New Hampshire could quickly dash any dream (or fantasy) of a move to 1600 Pennsylvania Avenue. But a methodical, coherent, intelligible nominating system—with the voters' interest and involvement the central concerns—would enhance how Americans make their decisions about the next president. The tumult and turmoil of the late 1960s unleashed forces that the national government now needs to tame and channel, in order to control a chaotic procedure possessing neither rhyme nor reason.

Back in 1983, the distinguished political scientist Nelson Polsby worried in his study *Consequences of Party Reform* that the growth of primaries might subordinate a candidate's abilities at executive leadership for the sake of other considerations, such as media savvy, charisma, and other image-oriented concerns. Writing shortly after Jimmy Carter's successful navigation of the more open nominating process and his much less successful presidency, Polsby noted "that there are some things that Presidents must do that people exposed to candidates only through the intermediation of the news media are unable to inform themselves about" (170). Performing well on television is one skill for an aspiring president, but it carries a politician just so far and is subordinate to making sound decisions affecting the executive branch and the nation, let alone the world. The following is even more relevant today than when Polsby wrote it in the early 1980s:

> If having the good opinion of colleagues and others intimately connected with government and politics means little or nothing to a candidate's chances for advancement, the nomination process then works at cross-purposes with the process of governing, which relies so heavily on accountability among elites. This may lead, in the first place, to inferior government, as persons unable to pass muster with their peers occasionally prove to be popularly attractive. In the second place, it may contribute to popular disaffection with government, as complaints about ineffective on-job performances filter down from Washington and interest group elites into the constituencies. (171)

Polsby died in 2007, but it's not difficult to predict what he'd say about Donald Trump winning the Republican nomination in 2016. Without experience in either governmental service or in the military, Trump also lacked "the good opinion of colleagues" in politics or government, as he went from state to state that winter and spring to compete in primaries and caucuses. He was still somehow able to prevail against sixteen other GOP candidates before defeating Hillary Clinton in the general election that fall, because the current system, political conditions, and media environment proved favorable to his unique personality and approach. Viewed in the round, and from a vantage point that allows for the most complete picture, Trump represents developments and new directions that have come into being as features of American democracy in recent decades. He's the epitome rather than the exception.

A structured, legislatively mandated process of regional primaries, which might involve officeholders who know the candidates well and can predict how they might perform in the White House, would bring a commonsense beginning to a presidential campaign. Nominating able and qualified men and women to campaign for the White House would ensure voters of a credible choice on Election Day. But what about also reconsidering how incumbents complete their service as chief executive and commander in chief? Is it time to consider repealing the Twenty-Second Amendment? The key passage in the amendment is its first sentence, which reads, "No person shall be elected to the office of the President more than twice, and no person who has held the office of President, or acted as President, for more than two years of a term to which some other person was elected President shall be elected more than once."

The amendment directly took on the thinking of Alexander Hamilton, who devoted two of *The Federalist Papers* (numbers 71 and 72) to the length of service for "the Executive." Writing as "Publius" on March 21, 1788—a little more than a year before Washington's first inauguration—Hamilton in number 72 addressed what he called "re-eligibility" of the president. Spelling out five specific "disadvantages which would flow from the principle of exclusion," Hamilton in his editorial explaining this aspect of the Constitution is definite in his opposition to preventing someone from continuing in office. In his opinion, voters engaged in the electoral process should make the decision—"to enable the people, when they see reason to approve of his [the president's] conduct, to continue him in his station, in order to prolong the utility of his talents and virtues, and to secure to the government the advantage of permanency in a wise system of administration." There's a certain irony that Hamilton, considered by many the grandfather of the Republican Party, saw no reason to restrict "the chief magistrate" to a fixed amount of time in office. Washington thought similarly, writing the Marquis de Lafayette a year before he was inaugurated in 1789 that "I can see no propriety in precluding ourselves from the services of any man, who on some great emergency shall be deemed universally most capable of serving the Public."

However, Washington's decision to return to Mount Vernon in 1797 after two four-year terms set a precedent, though an informal one, that was (more or less) observed for nearly a century. Interestingly another war hero, Ulysses S. Grant, tried to return to the White House in the 1880 election—he had been president from 1869 until 1877—but he lost on the thirty-sixth ballot at the Republican convention to James A. Garfield, the fall campaign's victor. Even more ostentatiously, Theodore Roosevelt challenged the Washingtonian way by mounting a third-party run in 1912, despite the fact that he had headed the Republican Party's national ticket only once: in 1904. (Since William McKinley was assassinated about six months into his second term in 1901, TR served all but 194 days of two complete terms.)

Roosevelt's custom-breaking ambition—TR, like Grant, wanted to return to office after one intervening term—must have given politicians of the time ideas. Woodrow Wilson, who defeated Roosevelt and Republican incumbent William Howard Taft in 1912, entertained the unrealistic fantasy of seeking a third term in both 1920 and 1924, even though he had suffered a crippling stroke in October 1919. Embarking on a political-governmental career in 1910 at the age of twenty-eight, Franklin Roosevelt, of course, conspicuously disturbed the two-term mindset, winning four straight White House elections—1932, 1936, 1940, and 1944. FDR's extraordinary success prompted the heavily Republican Congress, which decisively won the 1946 midterm elections in the House and the Senate, to initiate the amendment process for restricting the presidency to a two-term maximum. GOP voting for approval was unanimous in both chambers, with some Democrats (including a recently elected member of the House from Massachusetts by the name of John F. Kennedy) also favoring the limitation. Most of the Democrats who voted with the Republicans were conservative Southerners and not exactly champions of the New Deal.

Article V of the Constitution stipulates that "two thirds of both Houses" of Congress or a constitutional convention called by two-thirds of state legislatures starts the procedure for amending the Constitution. The president has no formal role at any time. Three-fourths of the states must ratify the amendment for it to be enacted, which in the case of the Twenty-Second occurred on February 27, 1951. As a result, the president became unique in the national government in relation to the time of service allowed. There are no term limits for members of the House of Representatives or for the Senate, and Supreme Court justices enjoy appointments to the bench until they die, resign, or face removal after impeachment by the House and conviction by the Senate—which has never happened in US history.

The two-term restriction imposes a definite, unduly predictable cycle of planning and action on an administration that can be detrimental to governing and advancing a policy agenda. Eight years sounds like a long time; however, each year tends to have its own rhythm that's largely imposed from the outside. As discussed previously, presidents try to get major legislative proposals passed by Congress early in their first term to take advantage of the so-called honeymoon period. (The irony of this situation is that a president's time of maximum influence occurs when the new chief executive has the least experience working with Congress, and presidential appointees are still in the process of being nominated and confirmed.) One year to eighteen months after the inauguration, thoughts in Washington on both ends of Pennsylvania Avenue turn to the upcoming midterm elections, traditionally at least a partial referendum on the White House, even though the president is not on the ballot. In the seventeen midterm elections since Eisenhower's time, including the one in 2018, the president's party has lost House seats fifteen times—as many as sixty-three in 2010 and fifty-two in 1994. (The average is between twenty-five and thirty.) For the Senate, there's greater stability because senators serve six-year terms; however, the incumbent president has seen a decline in his party's numbers twelve of the seventeen times since 1954. Strikingly, the largest setbacks—Republicans lost thirteen senators in 1958 and Democrats nine in 2014—took place during the second terms of Eisenhower and Obama.

A president's first midterm leads almost directly to focused planning for a reelection campaign in two years. Beginning with Eisenhower, every incumbent president, with the exception of Johnson in 1968, has campaigned to remain in office. Six of the nine won a second term—Eisenhower, Nixon, Reagan, Clinton, George W. Bush, and Obama. Ford (never elected on a national ticket), Carter, and George H. W. Bush were all defeated within a sixteen-year period.

White House reelection, however, leads fairly quickly to the perception by those in Congress that a lame duck is making the decisions in the Oval Office. In 2005, with solid Republican majorities in both the House and the Senate, George W. Bush proposed reforming Social Security and traveled around the country for town hall meetings, to explain a system featuring partial privatization. Despite the considerable investment of political capital that he said he had earned with his reelection victory, Bush's initiative never reached the floor of Congress. After Democrats gained control of both the House and the Senate in the midterm elections of 2006, the Bush administration's legislative agenda became, to be kind, modest.

Obama faced similar roadblocks during his second term, voicing the following in a cabinet meeting in 2014:

> We're not just going to be waiting for legislation in order to make sure that we're providing Americans the kind of help they need. I've got a pen and I've got a phone. And I can use that pen to sign executive orders and take executive actions and administrative actions that move the ball forward in helping to make sure our kids are getting the best education possible, making sure that our businesses are getting the kind of support and help they need to grow and advance, to make sure that people are getting the skills that they need to get those jobs that our businesses are creating.

Obama signed forty-nine executive orders in his final months as president, but his attempt to have a Supreme Court justice confirmed by the Senate during his last White House year got nowhere.

Would the possibility of seeking a third term (or even potentially more) help a president perform the job he—or she—is elected to do? Since the 1950s, second terms have been fraught with dangers and difficulties. Remember, specifically, the scandal involving Sherman Adams and the U-2 affair for Eisenhower, Watergate for Nixon, the Iran-Contra imbroglio for Reagan, the impeachment of Clinton, and so on. A Gallup study comparing first- and second-term average approval numbers for recent presidents who served the full eight years is revealing (see Table 1). Three of the five decline in the public's judgment, and Clinton's rise, in large measure, can be attributed to a backlash against the Republican House for the impeachment proceedings of 1998. As discussed previously, Clinton registered his highest approval, 73 percent, in December 1998, the month he was impeached. Citizens who were surveyed sent a definite message with a dual meaning: approval of the president's governmental performance *and* disapproval of the way he was treated by independent counsel Kenneth Starr and Congress.

Table 1. Presidential approval numbers in first and second terms.

President	First Term	Second Term
Eisenhower	69.6%	60.5%
Reagan	50.3%	55.3%
Clinton	49.6%	60.6%
G. W. Bush	62.2%	36.5%
Obama	49.1%	46.7%

Repealing the Twenty-Second Amendment would keep a president's political antennae acute and more sensitive to the implications of decision making. Moreover, members of the House and Senate would be more inclined to work with a president (not assumed to be on the way out) as a governmental partner, whose power would remain more constant throughout each term. What has become a predictable second-term slump might dissipate if an incumbent were seriously looking ahead to another campaign. And keeping Congress and the public wondering about whether a president would stay in office would invigorate the executive branch—and the news media. The era of journalists refusing to cover the health of a president is over, and there would be no way the frailty of someone (such as FDR in 1944) would go unnoticed by reporters assessing the merits of all the candidates. Even should a president decide not to seek a new term, why not delay that announcement to a year or so before the next election?

Doing away with the Twenty-Second Amendment is by no means an original suggestion. Repeal proposals come up from time to time, often as resolutions originating in the House or Senate. Since its ratification, several prominent Democrats and Republicans have pointed out the hazards that exist when a president's service is limited by law. One of the most cogent and persuasive statements came from Harry Truman, when he appeared before a Senate subcommittee on constitutional amendments near the end of Eisenhower's second term (on May 4, 1959). Plain spoken and direct as usual, the former president opined in the second sentence of his remarks that this "bad amendment . . . ought to be repealed." Reaching back to the Constitutional Convention debate and the decision *not* to limit the time a president serves, he contrasted "how wise the framers" were compared to "the Roosevelt haters," who "sold the country a bill of goods." Truman then considered the present-day circumstances and the consequences of the amendment on the current president and his successors. His points, presented in the gender-specific language of the time, yet even more provocative now than six decades ago, merit extended quotation and this generation's deliberation:

> It is ironic that the first "lame duck" President to be hamstrung by this Amendment is one of the Republicans' own.
>
> This brings me to an overriding reason for repealing the 22nd Amendment, a reason which was not fully developed in the original Constitutional debates. During the years since the Convention of 1787, the Presidency of the United States has grown into the most important office in the history of the world. The welfare, not only of this country, but of the whole world depends on how effectively the duties of that office can be discharged. The job is an almost impossible one under any circumstances—the man who holds it needs all the prestige, all the position of leadership, that is possible. This is not for his aggrandizement and glory but for the welfare of all of us.
>
> You don't have to be very smart to know that an office holder who is not eligible for re-election loses a lot of influence. So, what have you done? You've taken a man and put him in the hardest job in the world, and sent him out to fight our battles in a life and death struggle—you've sent him out to fight with one hand tied behind him because everyone knows he can't run for re-election.
>
> It makes no sense to treat a President this way—no matter who he is—Republican or Democrat. He is still the

President of the whole country; and all of us are dependent on him; and we ought to give him the tools to do the job.

If he is not a good President, and you don't want to keep him, you don't have to re-elect him. There is a way to get rid of him and it does not require a Constitutional Amendment.

Ronald Reagan had reservations similar to those of his predecessor and fellow midwesterner by birth. While serving his second term, he began to talk about initiating a movement to repeal the Twenty-Second Amendment after he left office. During one of his last interviews as president in 1989, he told Tom Brokaw of NBC News why he thought it was necessary to amend the amendment by ending it: "This is the only office that is elected by all the people. I think that is an infringement on the democratic rights of the people. . . . It is an invasion of their democratic rights to vote for whoever they want to vote for and for however long."

More recently, Representative Steny Hoyer, a Democrat from Maryland, and Senator Mitch McConnell, a Republican from Kentucky, have sponsored bills advocating an end to the amendment, which has affected five twice-elected presidents (Eisenhower, Reagan, Clinton, George W. Bush, and Obama) during nearly seven decades. McConnell, who as of this writing is the Senate majority leader, is an opponent of term limits for anyone in an elected national office: House, Senate, and White House. In 1995, with his party in control of both congressional chambers, yet with a Democrat (Clinton) at 1600 Pennsylvania Avenue, McConnell maintained that the Twenty-Second Amendment was "a brash, ill-conceived, hastily executed and strictly partisan response to the unprecedented tenure of President Roosevelt. As constitutional scholars have observed, this was the first constitutional modification that constricted voter suffrage. And Republicans should take heed, for it is we who have been hoisted by their petard. It is poetic justice, in a sense, that Presidents Eisenhower and Reagan are the only ones, thus far, who have been constrained. . . . It would be fitting, and in the national interest, for the Republican majority of 1995 to rectify a mistake made by the Republican majority of 1947" (*Congressional Record*, January 24, 1995). Though respected Democrats and Republicans have offered well-reasoned appeals for repeal, their words have never resulted in action. In the polarized political environment that has developed in recent decades, the possibility of passing a constitutional amendment seems fanciful. Amendments must be ratified by a two-thirds' majority in both the Senate and the House, after which the legislatures of three-fourths (thirty-eight) of the fifty states must vote for ratification. The last amendment to be formally approved (the Twenty-Seventh, which concerned congressional salaries) took almost 203 years to become law. It was ratified on May 5, 1992, after being submitted on September 25, 1789. (That is a long story in itself.) By contrast, four amendments were added to the Constitution between 1961 and 1971.

To make sure that there's no suggestion of America becoming a nation where a president could be elected for life, why couldn't there be a constitutional amendment stating that a "natural born Citizen" who is seventy-five years old or older is not eligible to seek the presidency? Article II, section 1 of the Constitution says that a candidate must "have attained to the Age of thirty five Years" to be able to serve. If there's a minimum age, why not a maximum for president—and possibly members of the House and Senate as well? Life expectancy back in the eighteenth century was about thirty-five years, according to one study, but today it is more than double that. Stipulating a specific upper-age limit for someone seeking "executive Power" wasn't even a consideration for the framers of the Constitution. (Interestingly, since William McKinley's first White House win, the average age of Republicans elected as president is 58.9 years, while it is 49.2 years for Democrats. These statistics do not include the ages of Theodore Roosevelt, Calvin Coolidge, Harry Truman, Lyndon Johnson, or Gerald Ford, all of whom became president directly from the vice presidency.)

In fact, James Monroe believed that establishing the minimum of thirty-five years helped avoid the possibility of dynastic succession involving a father and a son. Explaining his interpretation of this portion of the Constitution, he wrote, "The Constitution has provided, that no person shall be eligible to the office, who is not thirty-five years old; and in the course of nature very few fathers leave a son who has arrived to that age." John Adams proved to be one of the "few fathers" that nature favored. He was eighty-nine in 1824, when John Quincy Adams was elected to the White House, and the senior Adams died on July 4, 1826, the same day as Thomas Jefferson, who was eighty-three.

Repealing the Twenty-Second Amendment wouldn't be easy, though another one (the Eighteenth establishing the prohibition of alcoholic beverages) was superseded with the ratification of the Twenty-First Amendment some thirteen years later. While abolishing or circumventing the Electoral College, spelled out in practice but not by name in section 1, article II of the Constitution, might be even more difficult to repeal, it too warrants the citizenry's serious reflection and debate.

Five times since the nation's founding—the 2016 election was the fifty-eighth since 1788—the winner of the popular vote has lost the Electoral College ballot and thus the presidency. Andrew Jackson in 1824, Samuel Tilden in 1876, Grover Cleveland in 1888, Al Gore in 2000, and Hillary Clinton in 2016 received more support from voters, respectively, than John Quincy Adams, Rutherford Hayes, Benjamin Harrison, George W. Bush, and Donald Trump. Both Jackson and Cleveland sought the White House four years later and triumphed—with Cleveland becoming the only president to serve nonconsecutive terms. For trivia aficionados, Cleveland won the popular vote in three straight national contests—as did Jackson before him. Franklin Roosevelt garnered the most votes four times.

Given the final outcomes in 2000 and 2016 (two of the most recent elections), it might be time to reconsider the democratic value of the Electoral College and the way it currently operates. Increasingly, modern White House campaigns are less national in scope and more do-or-die clashes in targeted battleground states, where there's the possibility of either party's candidate winning. This means that sophisticated computer studies identify the most competitive places that deserve a candidate's time, attention, and financial resources. The rest of America doesn't see or hear the country's potential leader except through the filter of the media, and a candidate's advertising reaches just the relatively few states—a dozen or so usually—being contested.

The last concerted effort to abolish the Electoral College and replace it with the direct, popular-vote election of the president took place in 1969 and 1970. Senator Birch Bayh of Indiana, the chairman of the Senate's Subcommittee on the Constitution and the lawmaker largely responsible for both the Twenty-Fifth (on presidential disability and succession) and the Twenty-Sixth (lowering the voting age to eighteen) Amendments, spearheaded adoption of yet another amendment, which would have mandated that victory on the national level, rather than in state-by-state contests, decide who occupies the White House. The House of Representatives supported the measure 339 to 70 on September 18, 1969, and President Richard Nixon endorsed the bill twelve days later; however, a Senate filibuster in September 1970 killed the measure, one of some seven hundred attempts in US history to modify or eliminate the Electoral College.

In 1978, the Twentieth Century Fund assembled a task force of respected scholars, political consultants, and journalists to analyze how presidents are elected with the purpose of proposing reforms to improve the process. The principal recommendation became what members of the committee called "the national bonus." The task force's published report, *Winner Take All*, explains the new procedure of "adding a national pool of electoral votes to the existing state pool of electoral votes. This national pool would consist of two electoral votes for each state (plus the District of Columbia), which would be awarded on a winner-take-all basis to the candidate with the most popular votes nationwide. The state and national pools of electoral votes would then be added together, and the candidate with the majority of electoral votes would be elected to the presidency." This new scheme would add 102 votes to the 538 that now make up the Electoral College, and a key virtue of this suggestion is that it tries to correct a problem, while recognizing past procedures. As the report argues, "The Task Force proposal would maintain the desirable features of the existing system *and* virtually assure that the winner of the popular vote in the nation will be the electoral vote winner." Like so many other reform ideas, this one died from neglect and lack of civic enthusiasm, if not interest.

Of late, however, there is a definite plan for change that is worthy of deliberation and discussion. It is called the National Popular Vote Interstate Compact, which—if approved by enough states—would ensure that the winner of the popular vote became president. States participating in the compact would promise to have their electors support the winner of the popular vote, regardless of how well that candidate did in the states that the electors represent. The Electoral College would continue to function as in the past, but the method of assigning a state's votes—the combination of the number of House districts and the two Senate seats—would change. It's something of an end-around maneuver to keep the Electoral College in place while also ensuring the candidate who collects the greatest number of individual votes wins the ultimate prize, a White House victory.

Since the compact was proposed in 2006, several state legislatures—including California, New York, and Illinois—have enacted its provisions, though at this writing not enough to reach a majority of the necessary electoral votes. To its credit, the proposal follows the Constitution's directive that states "shall appoint, in such Manner as the Legislature thereof may direct, a Number of Electors." Working through the legislatures of individual states is the key; however, abandonment of procedures that date back to the country's earliest days won't occur without agitated, protracted argument, education, and persuasion.

Proponents of the compact no doubt will contend that presidential campaigns would be more democratic, more of an expression of the will of the voting majority, while opponents will assert that candidates, instead of focusing on particular states for their electoral votes, would concentrate their time and advertising on gaining support in cities and surrounding areas with large populations. Since Clinton defeated George H. W. Bush in 1992, Republicans have won the popular vote just once (2004) in the last seven elections but have prevailed in the Electoral College three times: 2000, 2004, and 2016. Democrats are bound to intensify their party's efforts to produce institutional or structural change if this trend continues in 2020 and beyond.

Once the Electoral College vote is official, a president—either new or incumbent—benefits from advice regardless of its origin. Public figures, civic leaders, business or subject specialists, and engaged citizens all can contribute ideas or suggestions of potential value to a president's thinking and to the discourse on behalf of the common good. One cohort with a unique perspective on the demands and difficulties of the office is former occupants of the White House. Ex-presidents rarely engage, with any degree of formality, in government business after their administrations end. John Quincy Adams won election to the House of Representatives in 1830, after losing the presidential campaign of 1828, and then served in Congress with distinction until his death in 1848. Another one termer, William Howard Taft, was confirmed as chief justice of the Supreme Court in 1921, eight years after his presidency. Though never elected president, Andrew Johnson completed Abraham Lincoln's second term and later won a US Senate seat from Tennessee, dying five months after beginning his service.

In the 1930s, as a senator, Harry Truman advocated that former presidents be allowed to speak in the Senate on legislative issues, a proposal that didn't get very far. He developed this idea more fully decades later in his book *Mr. Citizen*, published in 1960. Now the former chief executive recommended that legislation be passed to designate "former Presidents of the United States as *Free Members of the Congress*" (123). According to this proposition, each "Free Member" would be able to sit on the floor of either the Senate or the House and engage in ongoing debates—but *not* have the right to vote on any legislation. This suggestion, however, never found a constituency of support.

Rather than thinking in terms of Congressional participation, it would be valuable, though, if there existed a Council of Presidents, which would meet four times each year with the incumbent occupant of the Oval Office to discuss problems and concerns facing the country. Especially at a time when American politics is so deeply divided and polarization is undeniable, the council's meetings could look beyond partisan differences to assess the contemporary world "steadily and . . . whole," as Matthew Arnold phrased it. Someone who has served as president knows the stakes involved in making major, often life-or-death decisions. The advantage to the sitting president and to the nation could be considerable—or, frankly, negligible—but the meetings themselves would have substantive and symbolic worth. Moments fostering national unity seem increasingly rare in America, and presidents share experiences only a handful of people have. Taxpayers are still supporting the former presidents with pensions and expense costs, and they already have exclusive use of the Presidential Townhouse in Washington. The Council of Presidents would formally create an advisory board, connecting the past and the present, that would also provide institutional continuity. As the genuine friendships between Gerald Ford and Jimmy Carter and between George H. W. Bush and Bill Clinton show, campaign rivals need not remain adversaries once an election is history. A former president has experience that's unique—and usable. John Kennedy consulted his predecessor, Dwight Eisenhower, during the Cuban Missile Crisis of 1962 and came away from the conversation with greater insight into what the Soviet Union might—or might not—do.

Discussions among members of the council would be off-the-record and remain confidential unless the members formally agreed to make particular discussions or policy reviews public. An incumbent president, however, does owe the public regularly scheduled, hour-long sessions with journalists to explain an administration's work and initiatives. Article II, section 3 of the Constitution mandates delivery to Congress of "Information of the State of the Union," which since Franklin Roosevelt's presidency has become the civic ritual of a speech to a joint session of Congress. One evening each year—Lyndon Johnson began the tradition of the prime-time address for maximum television viewership in 1965—a president commands the attention of House and Senate members, as well as anywhere from thirty to sixty million people in the television audience at home, according to Nielsen statistics. Nobody objects to one late January night being devoted to a ceremonial and formal report to the nation from the president, though the now-common practice of legislators acting like wide-eyed children asking for autographs from the leader of the executive branch borders on the ridiculous and reduces the occasion's decorum.

But what about other times during the year? According to the American Presidency Project, both Calvin Coolidge and Franklin Roosevelt conducted over 70 news conferences per year during their White House days, more than one each week. The average began to decline with Harry Truman (41.73 annually), and then fluctuated at well below three per month as these yearly averages show—Eisenhower, 24.13; Kennedy, 22.89; Johnson, 26.16; Nixon, 7.03; Ford, 16.32; Carter, 14.75; Reagan, 5.75; Bush senior, 34.25; Clinton, 24.13; Bush junior, 26.25; and Obama, 20.38. Though Trump appears frequently in front of cameras, he tends to respond to a few questions, often side-by-side with foreign leaders, rather than engage in full-scale news conferences. Occasions beyond scripted speeches, Twitter tidings, and brief media exchanges would give the public a better sense of Trump as president.

A monthly news conference or interview would, for example, allow a president to discuss pending legislation, administration proposals, and current squabbles with Congress. One month there could be a regular session with White House journalists. Another time might feature the principal news anchors of the television networks. The next opportunity might include three or four prominent columnists. In short, the format could change throughout the year to sustain public interest, and some meetings might even feature questions from the public. The United Kingdom's House of Commons features Prime Minister's Questions each Wednesday for thirty minutes or so when Parliament is in session. This proposal is for the president to do something similar, though it would be monthly, not weekly; would be a full hour in length; and would be conducted by the news media. Just as televised debates between presidential candidates have over time become significant moments during the fall campaign cycle, the country's leader should come before the public frequently to make the case for the administration. In fact, "Will you tonight promise—and commit yourself—to a monthly session to answer questions from journalists and citizens, if you are elected president?" could be asked of presidential candidates at debates. If a candidate declined to pledge involvement in recurring question-and-answer sessions, voters could take this rebuff of public accountability into consideration when casting their votes.

Institutional change, especially when it entails amending the Constitution or passing new legislation, won't happen without enormous effort. Someone, for instance, musing even vaguely about seeking the White House might be reluctant to propose (or endorse) any reforms related to an office to which the man or woman aspires. Self-interest trumps the public interest almost every time. But the presidency will be made stronger by refining some of the procedures and practices now in effect. Comprehensible reform that helps to involve and illuminate the public in a thorough, fair-minded way will position the nation's highest office to meet challenges of the twenty-first century.

During the past five decades, influential book-length studies have identified "the imperial presidency," "the rhetorical presidency," and "the imperiled presidency." With the White House buffeted by an array of challenges and profound change, it is necessary for those working in politics and for citizens engaged in self-government to seek men and women with leadership experience, skill, and capacity to produce an "effective presidency" of idealistic (yes, at times, partisan) principle, pragmatic judgment, and unambiguous decisiveness in equal measure. Any lectern adorned with the presidential seal is "a bully pulpit" for inspiring the public and advocating for causes that might improve the commonweal. But communication, however bully, is never enough. It's the day-to-day, dawn-to-nightfall work of governing—with knowledge and foresight—that results in an institution, of singular importance, closer to what the founders envisioned and to what so many Americans yearn for today.

— S I X —

Presidency in Progress

Since the 2016 Election Day, I have tried, however inadequately, to interpret the victory of Donald J. Trump and his early period as president in various venues, both academic and popular. This chapter brings together reporting and analysis from lectures delivered at the University of Innsbruck (December 13, 2016; May 16, 2018) and at Dublin City University (September 20, 2017), as well as portions of articles that appeared in the Review section of the Irish Independent *(November 12, 2016; August 5, 2017; November 4, 2017; January 20, 2018; October 13, 2018). I am grateful to Professor Gudrun Grabher at the University of Innsbruck; Professor Gary Murphy at Dublin City University; and Catherine O'Mahony and Rachel Dugan, both at the* Irish Independent, *for providing occasions to talk and to write about the current occupant of the White House.*

This chapter was submitted to the publisher in early 2019, with several investigations of President Trump and his administration at various stages of completion. By the time this book appears, some points of interpretation might deserve revision or emendation. One can hope, however, that the thrust of the analysis places the Trump presidency in its historical and institutional contexts at a moment like no other in US history.

The election of Donald J. Trump in 2016 caught most Americans—and people elsewhere—off guard. Final polls and best-guess predictions almost uniformly projected a victory by Hillary R. Clinton. The Real Clear Politics average of the last eleven surveys gave Clinton an edge of 3.3 percent over Trump—45.5 to 42.2—with just one tracking poll showing a two-point advantage for the Republican. The actual vote count gave Clinton 48.2 percent to Trump's 46.1, a spread of 2.1 percent and just short of most survey expectations.

With voter alienation palpable and antipathy to politics as usual at its angriest apotheosis, a novice candidate defied most conventions, traditions, and norms to capture the White House. Trump collected 77,744 more votes in the three key states of Michigan, Wisconsin, and Pennsylvania, thus winning the Electoral College and denying Clinton the presidency, despite her popular-vote advantage of 2,868,691 out of almost 137 million ballots cast. Michigan and Pennsylvania had gone Democratic the previous six presidential elections and Wisconsin the previous seven. In the all-important Electoral College, Trump prevailed 304 to 227, with seven "faithless electors" deciding not to support the candidates winning their states.

At his final campaign rally during the early morning hours of Election Day on November 8, Trump told a crowd in Michigan, "If we don't win, this will be the single greatest waste of time, energy, and money in my life." That one sentence of the zillion he spoke from the day he announced his candidacy on June 16, 2015, represents the essence of Trump's political, and personal, approach. For him, the personal and the political had become (and today remain) indistinguishable. Combining the "we" and "my" cleverly maintains his dual perspective. While appealing to supporters—in his often-repeated phrase "the forgotten men and women of our country"—Trump remained in the forefront ("my life") and wasn't shy in viewing matters related to him in the superlative ("single greatest"). Those linguistic formulations—and the psychological motivation propelling them—have roots in his formative days as a real estate developer-cum-media celebrity back in the 1970s. Since then, focusing on the first person and all the superlatives with which he believes he's associated became second nature to Trump, which, to be sure, his presidential candidacy and occupancy of the White House magnified to the millionth power.

Without a nanosecond of public service in his personal history, the victor in 2016 benefited from an electorate so jaundiced about Washington and its political machinations that a why-not candidate seemed reasonable to his 62,984,825 voters. Just before Election Day, the *New York Times* and CBS News conducted a poll that asked whether "the 2016 presidential campaign made you feel more excited or more disgusted about American politics?" Thirteen percent answered "excited," while 82 percent responded they were "disgusted." In words rather than numbers, the American body politic is suffering from multiple maladies—debilitating partisanship, toxic money, irrational candidate selection, and all the rest. Maybe someone lacking any prior experience deserved a chance. For many voters, what Trump said to African American audiences possessed a broader meaning beyond the racial constituency to whom he directed his question: "What the hell do you have to lose?"

Trump voters went to the polls with elevated blood pressure and hopes for radical change. Anger was a primary propulsion fuel. In the large-scale exit poll conducted on Election Day, almost a quarter of respondents (23 percent) said they were "angry" at the federal government. Trump won 75 percent of them to Clinton's 18. Nearly half the people surveyed—46 percent—reported being "dissatisfied" with the federal government. Trump carried that group, too. When 69 percent of the electorate is either angry or dissatisfied, as was the case in 2016, the winds of change are blowing at gale force against the establishment, the status quo, and the political elite: everything Clinton personified.

On November 18, 2016, in a speech to the Federalist Society's National Lawyers Convention, Nikki Haley, the South Carolina governor, who served as Trump's ambassador to the United Nations until 2019, described what occurred with an open-eyed realism not often heard in spin-driven postmortems: "If we as Republicans are going to lead effectively and have staying power as the governing party, we must accept that Donald Trump's election was not an affirmation of the way Republicans have conducted themselves. He ran against both parties, against a political system he argued was fundamentally broken, an argument the voters subscribed to in massive numbers. They rejected the political class of all stripes, Republicans included, and we have no one to blame but ourselves." Haley's assessment attaches informed, ground-level analysis to the exit poll. Throughout the nominating contests and the general election campaign, Trump took advantage of the sour civic mood and exploited the weaknesses of a process remarkably vulnerable to abuse and misuse. In his acceptance speech at the Republican National Convention in Cleveland, he boasted, "Nobody knows the system better than me, which is why I alone can fix it. I have seen firsthand how the system is rigged against our citizens, just like it was rigged against Bernie Sanders—he never had a chance." In those two sentences, you see why Trump appealed to the angry and dissatisfied to the degree that he did. What he said drew attention to his personal abilities with laser intensity while also delivering a more comprehensive criticism against the established political structure that killed off the insurgent dreams of his opponent's chief competitor. Right up until Election Day, Trump railed that electoral levers were "rigged" against him, embittering his followers about the evils of contemporary politics even more throughout the fall.

Besides his constant criticism of the way Washington works, Trump used his wealth to his advantage, traveling everywhere on his Boeing 757 or his Sikorsky S-76 helicopter. Of even greater value, however, was his expertise at commanding media attention, especially on television. In his book *Enemy of the People*, Marvin Kalb observes that ABC, CBS, and NBC "twisted their rules to show as much of Trump as they could, all to his political advantage. Because Trump was so unusual a political character, he attracted eyeballs and boosted network ratings, and the three networks made a lot of money" (17). The *Tyndall Report* computed that Trump received 1,144 minutes of coverage on the nightly newscasts of the trio, while Clinton appeared for 506 minutes, less than half that of her opponent. More broadly, according to mediaQuant, a firm that quantifies the "earned media" that a person or organization receives, Trump collected 647 million media mentions—online, broadcast, in blogs, on Twitter, and in print—in 2016 for a whopping media value of $4.96 billion. Clinton's value was $3.24 billion, and the firm's analysis explained the considerable imbalance: "Trump outpaced Clinton *in every media segment*, earning 53% more media value overall, with the starkest percent difference coming from Twitter with 142% more media value." (According to the Center for Responsive Politics, Clinton actually spent $768 million and Trump almost $398 million in their campaigns, with Clinton spending considerably more than Trump on television advertising.)

Like Barack Obama in 2008, Trump became the beneficiary of extensive media coverage early in the campaign because of the distinctive, newsworthy nature of his candidacy. Both Obama and Trump, though for quite different reasons, provided the media with new story lines that journalists could develop. Obama was the first minority candidate with a chance of winning, and his personal background—birth in Hawaii, youth in Indonesia, Ivy League education, involvement in Illinois state politics—opened doors to a life unlike that of most mainstream politicians. Trump, too, defied established stereotypes, using his media savvy to promote attention on himself to an extent that eluded other candidates. For instance, he was allowed to schedule phone interviews for disembodied appearances on the major networks' Sunday morning public affairs programs during the first months of the campaign. Producers and anchors understood Trump would spike interest for the show, whatever he might say. Media bias, always a tricky, complicated subject, often favors the new and different without partiality to party or ideology. Both Obama and Trump enjoyed a boost in coverage as they became identified as candidates with unique narratives compared to their opponents. (In 2008, according to the *Tyndall Report*, Obama received 745 minutes of coverage on the nightly news programs of ABC, CBS, and NBC. Four years later, when he'd become well known, it was just 157 minutes.)

To underestimate the power of personality in today's politics can prove fatal to those who think otherwise. Back in 1980, Democrats drooled at the prospect of a former actor, Ronald Reagan, running as the Republican presidential candidate against the incumbent Jimmy Carter. As it turned out, Reagan carried forty-four states and amassed ten times Carter's Electoral College total: 489 to 49. In 2016, Clinton campaign workers looked down their collective noses at a political rookie with abundant flaws and mused about where they would be working in the executive branch. As in 1980, reality overwhelmed misplaced expectations.

At rallies, in debates, during television interviews, and constantly on Twitter, Trump projected personal strength (usually invoking superlatives), delivered simplistic policy solutions (often in bombastic language), and conveyed a sense of command (complete with belittling nicknames and put-downs for opponents), which taken together created the argument that nobody was worthy of his challenge. He stood out by emphasizing his unique personality and the magic tricks of celebrity. Though new to the hurly-burly of politics, Trump in previous years had mastered the art of performance and learned how to stay in the media spotlight to keep the flame of fame aglow for as large a public as possible. In a 1990 interview with *Playboy* magazine, he admitted that his ostentatious displays of wealth—towering buildings, massive casinos, custom-fitted jets and yachts— served as "props for the show." The interviewer was intrigued and wondered: "And what is the show?" Without skipping a beat, the tycoon—described in the article's headnote as a "43-year-old billionaire"—replied, "The show is 'Trump' and it is sold-out performances everywhere."

Interestingly, during that same interview, politics, the presidency, trade, even nuclear war ("It's a very important element in my thought process.") come up. Never short of confidence, Trump, when the possibility of serving as president is raised, says, "I'd do the job as well as or better than anyone else," noting in the next exchange with the interviewer, "I don't want to be President. I'm one hundred percent sure. I'd change my mind only if I saw this country continue to go down the tubes." Two years before sitting down with *Playboy*, Trump's name entered the political rumor mill as one of several potential vice-presidential candidates to run with George H. W. Bush on the 1988 Republican ticket. In 1999, he even created an exploratory committee to consider becoming the Reform Party's standard-bearer in 2000, but he decided against pursuing that possibility. Though his name kept popping up politically, it wasn't until he raised doubts concerning Barack Obama's place of birth in early 2011 that observers sensed he was becoming more serious about public affairs. By waiting to become involved until the 2016 campaign, he knew that the Republican competition for the nomination would be wide open—and that there wouldn't be an incumbent at the top of the Democratic ticket.

Before deciding to enter politics, Trump continued to develop real estate projects and dramatized himself as wealth personified. Emphasizing his showmanship whenever possible, he even became a prime time television celebrity in 2004, with the debut of the reality show *The Apprentice*. Trump played himself as a successful executive, who judged business talent and called the shots in a series that aired for an amazing fourteen seasons as either *The Apprentice* or *The Celebrity Apprentice*. (To a certain extent, when you think about it, he was portraying a glorified game show host.) The first year, viewership was high—over 20 million in the weekly audience, with the grand finale drawing an impressive 28.1 million watchers.

For over a decade, though viewers kept declining, Trump projected himself as decisive and in command. During this time, the detail-preoccupied builder moved away from day-to-day construction ventures, to parlaying his name as a brand for enterprises of one kind or another, to appearing in the media in a variety of roles: host, guest, cameo walk-on, comic performer at professional wrestling matches, or whatever. For people beyond Manhattan's boldface-type tabloid columns, Trump became a well-known figure of Olympian vanity, and that familiarity helped lead to political popularity among "the forgotten men and women" of 2016. He kept telling them, as well as others in his electoral base, "I am your voice."

Campaign rallies featuring statements that were one part policy message and another part crowd-pleasing entertainment kept the faithful energized and amused. He knew exactly what he was doing—and shrewdly continued to schedule such events after his inauguration on January 20, 2017. In auditoriums and arenas, in which there was standing room only, he continued to be the focus of attention in freewheeling, feisty, and funny ways. As often as four times a week during the 2018 midterm campaign, the president departed Washington to fly to a strategically selected city with a competitive Senate or governor's race. Amid a carnival-like atmosphere, hawkers outside peddled hats, t-shirts, buttons, and other political paraphernalia. It was as though the circus had come to town.

To watch Trump at a political rally, with him in the starring role, is to see someone totally in his element and very much at home. The figure behind the brand-name buildings and products, who parlayed that business background into reality TV celebrityhood, commands the stage for over an hour. At these largely unscripted events, and without the pomp and circumstance of a band playing "Hail to the Chief," he brags, jokes, fulminates, pontificates, assails, and swaggers. Every accusation of "fake news" leads to clenched-fist fury directed at the press area, while mentions of Hillary Clinton automatically trigger chants of "Lock her up, lock her up." For a congenital showman, who is also a teetotaler, all the cheering is a hundred-proof elixir. Part political pep talk and part ego trip, a Trump rally has entertainment value that far exceeds any serious disquisition on policy or the state of contemporary politics. Well-received routines from 2016 come back to life at these performances, where he often *plays* at being presidential, mocking the formality and ceremony of the office George Washington, Abraham Lincoln, and Franklin Roosevelt once occupied. He is simultaneously outrageous and pugnacious—and the audience loves both the act and the actor.

Trump's orientation to stagecraft, often at the expense of statecraft, is a sine qua non in understanding his conduct as president. On December 9, 2017, shortly before Trump completed his first year in the White House, he was the subject of a lengthy article in the *New York Times* that ran under the headline "Inside Trump's Hour-by-Hour Battle for Self-Preservation." A key paragraph reports, "Before taking office, Mr. Trump told top aides to think of each presidential day as an episode in a television show in which he vanquishes rivals. People close to him estimate that Mr. Trump spends at least four hours a day, and sometimes as much as twice that, in front of a television, sometimes with the volume muted, marinating in the no-holds-barred wars of cable news and eager to fire back."

The values of television often dictate what he says and does. Bold, attention-grabbing statements (e.g., missile threats from North Korea "will be met with fire and fury like the world has never seen") and constant combat, whether against Democrats, the news media, or the "deep state" of government bureaucracy, keep the unfolding narrative of the Trump presidency front and center. As a result, it often becomes difficult to remember and keep straight all the players, plotlines, twists, and turns. Planned and unplanned diversions always lead the public to focus on the political protagonist.

To compare quotidian activities in the White House to a continuing reality show would not contort credulity. The following are on display for all to see:

- Distinctive, sometimes incredible characters, with vivid personalities
- Dramatic conflict of one kind or another with constant tension
- Animated dialogue among principal characters, keeping on-lookers wondering what else might be said
- Rapid plot changes involving the characters, with some getting fired and losing their roles
- A pervasive sense of volatility, even chaos, heightening the "reality" and making the media and public speculate about the next move in the always-evolving political drama

In this media-driven milieu, governing is less scripted and more spontaneous. The on-again, off-again, on-again summit involving the president and North Korean leader Kim Jong Un in June 2018 exemplifies the reality show formula and how it can play out in high-stakes international negotiations. From being dismissed by Trump as "Little Rocket Man" and as "a madman" in fall 2017, the absolute ruler of the hermit kingdom subsequently grew in stature (becoming "very honorable" in a Trump description six months later) and earned a meeting with the leader of the free world on June 12, 2018. The path to the summit included several detours and corkscrew turns before the discussions took place in Singapore, with each hiccup along the way heard 'round the world.

After the relatively short interaction between Trump and Kim, the president often referred to the success of his initiative, saying in an interview on *60 Minutes* that aired October 14, 2018, that "the day before I came in, we were going to war with North Korea. I think it was going to end up in war." Then he elaborated, "We were going to war with North Korea. Now you don't hear that. You don't hear any talk of it. And he [Kim] doesn't want to go to war, and we don't want to go to war, and he understands denuclearization and he's agreed to it."

Trump was more clever and colorful in discussing United States–North Korean relations during a campaign rally in West Virginia two weeks earlier:

I was really being tough [with Kim], and so was he. I would go back and forth and then we fell in love. Okay. No, really! He wrote me beautiful letters. And they're great letters. We fell in love. Now they'll say [here he assumes the persona of a serious television anchor]: "Donald Trump said they fell in love. How horrible, how horrible is that? So unpresidential!" And I always tell you, it's so easy to be presidential. But instead of having 10,000 people outside trying to get into this packed arena, we'd have about 200 people standing right there. It's so easy to be presidential.

Given the unusual and unorthodox nature of this unique presidency, how can an average American, who is not blindingly partisan or ideological, interpret Donald Trump as a politician and public official? Any explanation begins with him. As far as he's concerned, as noted before, the personal is indeed political—with even a muted critique an affront and a challenge to him as an individual and to his authority. No shot goes unanswered; every punch is countered by another, usually of greater force. Being constantly combative was Trump's fists-up approach in the New York tabloid environment, where he battled for attention as a figure of wealth, fame, and influence. Back then, the coverage of the developer-celebrity was mostly on *his* terms. He was well known and certainly public but also secretive, controlling how he was portrayed as much as he could. Media melees before 2015 resembled professional wrestling matches and tended to be Gotham-centric.

Trump's relationship with journalists began to change, first after he became a serious candidate and later as the president. Increasingly, his past and how he handled the present turned into fair game, and the coverage often proved too critical for his taste. His stock response to any story he perceived as negative never wavered from blanket denial. The report was fabricated or fictional, he would assert, judgments he unfailingly transmitted via Twitter and elsewhere. Long-time allies in promoting him, the media, except for partisan outlets, seemed to change sides, with Trump now denouncing any faultfinding that came to his attention. But taking on foes comes naturally to this president and also serves a larger purpose.

Although his reaction to any challenge continues to be principally personal, it is perceived by his core constituency as also fighting on *their* behalf, especially when he attacks his and their common enemies—political opponents, government bureaucrats, or virtually anyone in mainstream journalism. In their eyes, Trump is taking on the status quo of "the Washington swamp" that they can't abide. The commander in chief wears another hat—"disrupter in chief"—which they also applaud, and any notion of decorum or acting in a "politically correct" fashion is well below a tertiary concern for them. The disrupter is at liberty to lash out at or to put down whoever intrudes on his work or agenda, the more assertively the better. (In his opponents' eyes, however, the disrupter in chief often assumes another, even more ominous role—destroyer in chief—imperiling traditions and norms of effective governance both domestically and internationally.)

Trump's nearly knee-jerk reliance on a combative, confrontational approach makes it difficult for him to switch gears when events dictate that a president should try to console or unify the country—say, after a natural disaster or after the all-too-frequent mass shootings. The ability to express empathy with sincerity and authenticity is a critical trait if a leader wants to maintain a strong human connection with the public at large. In Trump's case, his blatant and satiric mockery of presidential protocol and past practices makes it difficult for him to fulfill the role of the nation's pastor and comforter. He was able to take advantage of political trends and patterns to win election. But once in office, he challenged its heritage and rituals by individualizing the presidency to an unprecedented degree.

Trump's conduct, especially what he says to the public and through social media, has become a topic of controversy in itself. In October 2018, when several packages carrying pipe bombs mailed to Trump critics were discovered and the deadly shooting in a Pittsburgh synagogue that claimed eleven lives took place a few days later, many political analysts wondered aloud whether the president's repeated emphasis on divisive issues could inflame certain people to engage in questionable or illegal acts. Trump curtly denied any role out of hand; however, Vice President Mike Pence provided a more fulsome denial: "Everyone has their own style, and frankly, people on both sides of the aisle use strong language about our political differences. But I don't think you can connect it to acts or threats of violence."

Ducking any suggestion of blame was, of course, the predictable response, but Trump offered few words of sympathy— and seemed more eager to appear at his previously planned campaign rallies for the 2018 midterm elections that were a few days away. In a commentary published in the *Washington Post* on October 28, Patti Davis, the daughter of Ronald and Nancy Reagan, contrasted how previous presidents had addressed tragedies with how Trump reacted. Her judgment, though certainly harsh, was formed on the basis of experience and what she had witnessed: "This president will never offer comfort, compassion, or empathy to a grieving nation. It's not in him. When questioned after a tragedy, he will always be glib and inappropriate. So I have a wild suggestion: Let's stop asking him. His words are only salt in our wounds."

Tellingly, when Trump decided to travel to Pittsburgh after the attack, congressional leaders, both Republican and Democratic, declined to accompany him, and the city's mayor urged the president to stay away. Some two thousand people protested the president's visit. Challenging norms and conventions is a double-edged sword and can lead anyone to question the appropriateness of a person's behavior in a situation that demands traditional decorum and protocol. It's possible an unabashed outsider to politics and government lacks the experience and understanding to recognize the larger purpose of conducting such formalities purposefully, as well as their symbolic resonance for a community and nation in a time of sorrow.

Whether he is responding without much emotion to a death, such as Senator John McCain's in 2018, or declining to throw out the first pitch on Opening Day of the baseball season, ceremonial occasions often seem foreign or even forbidden affairs for Trump. Where he doesn't go makes a statement of its own, and he forgoes opportunities that national moments create to transcend partisanship, if only for a brief time. While previous presidents of both parties were welcome to attend the celebration for the Kennedy Center Honors, Trump's possible attendance was criticized in both 2017 and 2018—and he didn't bother to go either time. He also broke with tradition those years and in 2019 by declining invitations to the White House Correspondents Association dinners. The ceremonial dimension of the presidency is a key component of serving as the head of state. However, that facet is in serious jeopardy if the occupant of the White House is—according to one article in the *Washington Post* published on August 28, 2018—"president non grata." Will Trump's quite deliberate emphasis on the personalization of the office become standard-operating procedure after he leaves office, or can Americans expect a return to the protocol and procedures that existed before 2017? To what extent do people worry about institutional traditions and whether they survive a period when they're not observed?

Trump's personality and way of acting magnify him in the public's eyes. He seems not only unavoidable but also transparent in the sense of being unambiguous—what we see is who he is. To be sure, he is impulsive, driven, mercurial, strong, narcissistic, hypersensitive, successful, temperamental, opinionated, and many other adjectives that supporters and antagonists could list. But he is also complicated, particularly in the paradoxes that contribute to the figure so visible and out front in business, television, and politics. The same person who doesn't miss a chance to attack a perceived adversary is first in line to object to criticism directed at him. The conspicuous business and political figure works overtime to be as inscrutable as possible concerning details of his deals, taxes, and private affairs. The duly-elected leader of what French intellectual Raymond

Aron called "the imperial republic" appears more at ease and at home with autocrats than with democrats on the world stage. The occupant of the White House takes pleasure in mocking the ceremonial traditions of the office he fought so hard to gain. The nation's governmental leader tweets personnel and policy changes before the people involved are informed of the president's decisions. Paradoxes keep appearing, adding to his complexity and his singularity.

One of the most intriguing aspects of Donald Trump is his identification with people different from him, particularly with respect to economic circumstances. In his 1990 interview with *Playboy*, he remarked, "If I ever ran for office, I'd do better as a Democrat than as a Republican—and that's not because I'd be more liberal, because I'm conservative. But the working guy would elect me. He likes me. When I walk down the street, those cabbies start yelling out their windows." Immediately after Trump's victory in 2016, Speaker of the House Paul Ryan observed, "Donald Trump heard a voice out in this country that no one else heard; he connected in ways with people no one else did; he turned politics on its head." Despite his affluence and prominence, Trump's "show"—first as entertainment and later as political communication—appealed more broadly than someone might have originally thought.

In the controversial and questionably sourced book *Fire and Fury: Inside the Trump White House* (2018), Michael Wolff relates this anecdote that has the ring of authenticity to it:

> Trump's understanding of his own essential nature was even more precise. Once, coming back on his plane with a billionaire friend who had brought along a foreign model, Trump, trying to move in on his friend's date, urged a stop in Atlantic City. He would provide a tour of his casino. His friend assured the model that there was nothing to recommend Atlantic City. It was a place overrun by white trash.
>
> "What is this 'white trash'?" asked the model.
>
> "They're people just like me," said Trump, "only they're poor." (23)

A more perceptive, indeed scholarly, analysis of Trump and his relationship to a key part of his base of political support appears in Amy Chua's study *Political Tribes: Group Instinct and the Fate of Nations* (2018):

> Race has split America's poor, and class has split America's whites. Even today, the tribal politics behind President Trump's election still baffles many. How could so many in America's working class have been "conned" by Trump? How can lower-income Americans possibly fail to see that Trump is not one of them?
>
> What these elites don't see is that Trump, in terms of taste, sensibilities, and values, actually *is* similar to the white working class. The tribal instinct is all about identification, and Trump's base identifies with him at a gut level: with the way he talks (locker room), dresses, shoots from the hip, gets caught making mistakes, and gets attacked over and over by the liberal media for not being politically correct, for not being feminist enough, for not reading enough books. His enemies, they feel, are their enemies. They even identify with his wealth, because that's what many of them want, along with a beautiful wife and big buildings with their names on them. For many working-class Americans, being antiestablishment is *not* the same as being antirich. (5)

Trump reinforces the identification and connection through constant communication with his core constituency of political support. He's not only disrupter in chief but also tweeter in chief—with Twitter his cyber soapbox for applauding advocates, defending himself, announcing policy, criticizing journalists, firing staff, and opining at will. Franklin Roosevelt, who once remarked that the presidency was "pre-eminently a place of moral leadership," mastered radio with his "Fireside Chats." John Kennedy and Ronald Reagan effectively projected national leadership via television. Obama sent out his first tweet as president on May 18, 2015, but Trump's continuous and intrepid use of Twitter will be his defining—and remembered—contribution to presidential communication in the first portion of the twenty-first century. For no cost and without great effort, he can circumvent the traditional media and deliver a message exactly as he desires to nearly sixty million followers. Twitter is Trump's high-tech megaphone or bullhorn—as well as his security blanket.

In his hands, this social medium, created in 2006, is something of a stream-of-consciousness script for the narrator-protagonist, who happens to occupy the highest political office in the United States—and the world. For many of Trump's most fervent defenders, punch-in-the-nose outbursts aimed at adversaries are both a form of entertainment—think professional wrestling—and a reassuring affirmation that the occupant of the White House isn't engaging in politics as usual. As with the people who loudly cheer at Trump's rallies (and there's no doubt overlap in the two groups), any lack of decorum or protocol pales in comparison to what neuroscientists call the "emotional arousal" from a Twitter zinger, especially an astringent one directed at a loathed enemy. Impulsiveness and an instinct for connecting with an audience find a perfect outlet with the verbal-shillelagh whack of a well-timed tweet. He's become commenter in chief.

Just as Trump understood how to appeal for the votes of the "forgotten men and women," he also realized that he needed a way to keep delivering messages on his terms without the filters of gatekeepers of any kind. In *The Trump White House: Changing the Rules of the Game* (2018), journalist and author Ronald Kessler draws from an interview he conducted with the president, who is portrayed quite favorably throughout the book, which serves as a reportorial counterpoint to *Fire and Fury.* "Without social media, I might not be here," Trump tells Kessler. "Because the news is so biased and so dishonest and so fake that without social media, I would have no way of fighting. I have way over a hundred million people when you add them all up. And I'm able to fight back because of social media. If I didn't have that, there'd be no way I could fight back the dishonesty of CNN and the dishonesty of ABC or CBS or NBC" (262). (It's revealing that all the news outlets singled out are television ones, and that he repeatedly emphasizes the importance of fighting.)

Trump's continuous use of social media, especially Twitter, as his cyber soapbox, keeps him at the center of attention, and what he says receives enormous amplification in the mainstream organizations he fulminates against but monitors closely. Singularity is an important characteristic in approaching Trump and his decision making. Cabinet and staff members come and go, but there's no doubt who is dictating all the changes. As was the case in his business career, in which he never had to answer to a board of directors, other people are involved in whatever he's doing, but they are minor, supporting characters to the main one, who is always the primary focus. The singularity principle that exists on a personal level—his self-absorption, often diagnosed as narcissism by psychologists, is oceanic, if not cosmic— also extends to policy. Trump regards multilateral agreements with suspicion or disdain, and that thinking extends to historical partnerships with traditional allies and friends. Withdrawing from the Paris Climate Accord in 2017, the Iran nuclear deal, and the United Nations Human Rights Council in 2018, as well as from various trade relationships, draws into question the value of alliances and, for better or for worse, fosters a go-it-alone strategy. According to this thinking, a populist "America First" nationalism has replaced globalization in Oval Office orientation, and one person (sitting at the Resolute desk) will make the deals *he* wants in *his* way.

Someone who always wants the last word and the final say will do whatever it takes to make a case and to combat opposing information and action. That is one reason why Trump sends out so many tweets asserting his viewpoint and the rationale for it. No critical slug at him or perceived slight is ignored, which means that the president often takes on the news media directly and in no uncertain terms. As mentioned in chapter 4, but which bears repeating with some elaboration, Trump first tweeted the phrase "FAKE NEWS"—in capital letters—on December 10, 2016, a month after his election. Since then, a day rarely passes without a complaint about news coverage appearing on his Twitter account or in statements he makes to the press. As noted previously, on February 17, 2017, the president went so far as to write, "The FAKE NEWS media (failing @nytimes, @NBC News, @ABC, @CBS, @CNN) is not my enemy, it is the enemy of the American People!" During his first year in the White House, according to one accounting, he used the word *fake* 404 times in his tweets or appearances: "fake news," "fake stories," "fake media," "fake polls," and so forth. Trump is savvy about the power of branding, as he demonstrated in his business dealings, and labeling what the citizenry reads and hears as "fake" undermines credibility and trust in whatever information is transmitted by traditional journalistic sources. That is the reason and the objective for the continuing drumbeat about "Fake News." On June 13, 2018, shortly after his day-long summit with Kim Jong Un in Singapore, he fired off this blistering tweet: "So funny to watch the Fake News, especially NBC and CNN. They are fighting hard to downplay the deal with North Korea. 500 days ago they would have 'begged' for this deal—looked like war would break out. Our Country's biggest enemy is the Fake News so easily promulgated by fools!"

Six weeks later (on July 24), Trump stood before the convention of the Veterans of Foreign Wars in Kansas City and stormed, "Don't believe the crap you see from these people—the fake news." After citing specific examples of coverage he found objectionable, he declared with a flourish, "And just remember: What you're seeing and what you're reading is not what's happening." The formulation of that stark admonition sent several analysts to hunt down a passage from George Orwell's novel *1984*: "The Party told you to reject the evidence of your eyes and ears. It was their final, most essential command." Reproducing Orwell's words produced an eerie echo to Trump's remarks in a setting much different (and more formal) than one of his political rallies.

Each assault on journalism chips away at the centuries-old premise that the news media play a necessary, indeed vital, role in democracy. Classic quotations about the relationship—from Thomas Jefferson to Edward R. Murrow—boil down to this: when the watchdog of government loses any of its bark or bite, the public—and the principle of self-governance—suffers. Trump's incessant criticism makes people question news itself, strengthening his own political position. Richard Nixon was a minor league player compared with Trump in denigrating the media and transforming his opprobrium into an ongoing rallying cry for his defenders. Even before Trump started on his campaign to marry *fake* and *news* in the public mind, he told the *60 Minutes'* correspondent Lesley Stahl, just before she started taping an interview, that attacking the media was a deliberate tactic. "'You know why I do it?'" Stahl quoted Trump as saying. "'I do it to discredit you all and demean you all so when you write negative stories about me, no one will believe you.'"

Trump knows exactly what he is doing. *Fake* and *false* go hand-in-hand, so the mainstream media are routinely rejected by those most loyal to the president—between 80 and 90 percent of self-identified Republicans, according to most surveys since his inauguration. In early 2018, the Gallup/Knight Foundation Survey on Trust, Media and Democracy was released. According to one finding, "Four in 10 Republicans consider accurate news stories that cast a politician or political group in a negative light to always be 'fake news.'" Another statistic showed that "on a multiple-item media trust scale with scores ranging from a low of zero to a high of 100, the average American scores a 37." According to the study, trust "is highly influenced by partisanship, with Democrats largely trusting the media and Republicans distrusting." A CBS News survey conducted in late July 2018 found that "strong Trump supporters" trust the president 91 percent of the time for "accurate information." The "mainstream media"? A measly 11 percent. This absence of consensus about the veracity of information means it is more difficult for the public to make judgments and form opinions about political issues and individuals, as truth gets jeopardized in the shuffle. The "fog of war" has moved from the battlefield of combat to daily democratic discourse, challenging the knowledge and understanding of citizens.

The constant conflict between the White House and news organizations means that journalists remain on a war footing in trying to cover Trump and his administration. One area of recurring focus is the number of inaccurate or misleading statements for which the president is directly responsible. Periodically, the *New York Times* publishes a list under the headline "Trump's Lies," quoting both direct statements made by the president and the accurate information that shows discrepancy between the two. In an accompanying article the first time the catalog appeared, the newspaper's headnote explained, "No other president—of either party—has behaved as Trump is behaving. He is trying to create an atmosphere in which reality is irrelevant." Moreover, the *Washington Post* keeps a tally of "false or misleading claims" made by Trump. Just before his 601st day in office in mid-September 2018, the paper counted over 5,000 such statements—an average of more than eight questionable assertions per day. By the end of October, the total had jumped to 6,420, an average of 30 per day during the rally-filled seven-weeks before the 2018 midterm election. By January 20, 2019, two years into the Trump presidency, the number stood at 8,158, according to the newspaper's Fact Checker department. In the article accompanying the database's accounting that appeared on January 21, 2019, in the *Post*, it was reported that "the president averaged nearly 5.9 false or misleading claims a day in his first year in office. But he hit nearly 16.5 a day in his second year, almost triple the pace."

For one story, which came out on June 1, 2018, the *Post* compared a Trump tweet that was sent May 31, 2018—"Not that it matters but I never fired James Comey because of Russia! The Corrupt Mainstream Media loves to keep pushing that narrative, but they know it is not true!"—to what the president told NBC News anchor Lester Holt on May 11, 2017: "I was going to fire Comey [the FBI director] knowing there was no good time to do it. And, in fact, when I decided to just do it, I said to myself, I said, you know, this Russia thing with Trump and Russia is a made-up story. It's an excuse by the Democrats for having lost an election that they should've won." The article goes on to quote what Trump told a visiting Russian delegation the day after the Comey firing on May 9, 2017: "I just fired the head of the FBI. He was crazy, a real nut job. I faced great pressure because of Russia. That's taken off." Contradictions are catnap to journalists—who are trained to record the exact statements of public figures and to be always on guard to point out rhetorical disparity. Given the centrality of Special Counsel Robert Mueller's investigation of possible Russian campaign involvement and related matters to Trump's self-regard (several tweets refer to the probe as "the single greatest witch hunt in American history"), is it any wonder why presidential inconsistency of this kind becomes news on its own? Of course, too, there's the exquisite irony of the person charging the media with manufacturing "fake news" being the promulgator of false information on a regular basis.

Determining the most accurate way to classify statements at variance with veracity, such as the tweet about Comey and Russia, depends on judgments related to intent, motivation, purpose, and memory. Spin, so much a part of political communication today, can involve deception, evasion, or distortion. By contrast, lying means to be deliberately dishonest, to spread falsehoods fabricated to misrepresent reality for a definite, premeditated reason. What Trump says is particularly difficult to categorize, because in his past life sticking to the facts and nothing but the facts was foreign to his experience in real estate. For instance, in the 1987 and 1988 best seller *Trump: The Art of the Deal*, written with Tony Schwartz, Trump brags, "I play to people's fantasies. People may not always think big themselves, but they can still get very excited by those who do. That's why a little hyperbole never hurts. People want to believe that something is the biggest and the greatest and the most spectacular."

Trump goes on to give his preferred mode of salesmanship a name: "truthful hyperbole," defining it as "an innocent form of exaggeration—and a very effective form of promotion" (58).

To put a few Trump Organization buildings in New York City to the stress test of factuality, Trump Tower was constructed with fifty-eight floors, but marketing brochures tout sixty-eight. Trump World Tower was built with seventy stories but is billed as having ninety. Trump International Hotel and Tower has forty-four floors yet advertises fifty-two. However, standard practice to boost big-city property ventures doesn't easily transfer to presidential pronouncements, of which every utterance, regardless of length, is scrutinized domestically and internationally for what it says—and doesn't say. Particularly with his Twitter blasts and his performances at campaign-style rallies, Trump's concern for accuracy in expression takes a backseat to delivering messages his supporters will cheer. Is it prevarication, or is it promotion? Is it even possible for someone in his seventies, whose entire life has involved playing to "people's fantasies" through personal showmanship, to change how he approaches communication and presents himself to the public? An observation made by journalist Salena Zito, writing in September 2016 for the *Atlantic,* became popular for explaining Trump's appeal in 2016: "The press takes him literally, but not seriously; his supporters take him seriously, but not literally." How should citizens, in general, deal with this new phenomenon, especially as they try to come to terms with complicated domestic and international affairs? Whom can we trust for facts and accurate information? Can "performance truth" (with blatant appeal to political supporters) coexist with "presidential truth" (with institutional ties to democratic judgments)?

Clearly the people who voted for Trump and continue to show their approval think one way, while others disagree, in some cases vehemently. Many in the president's core constituency applaud his results. Domestically, his administration receives credit for lowering taxes, strengthening immigration policies, reversing environmental regulations, nominating conservative judges, and reforming trade practices. Internationally, the threat from ISIS (the Islamic State of Iraq and Syria) has been reduced, Jerusalem is now officially the capital of Israel in America's eyes, and the possibility for nuclear-armed conflict on the Korean Peninsula seems (for the time being, at least) more remote. Action, the business of government, trumps words in their political calculus, with a frequently repeated slogan a Trumpian mantra: "Promises Made. Promises Kept." Former Oklahoma senator Tom Coburn, a Republican, spoke for more than himself when he admitted to a reporter, "We have a leader who has a personality disorder, but he's done what he actually told the people he was going to do, and they're not going to abandon him."

One of the shrewdest and most perceptive observers of Trump and his appeal is essayist Joseph Epstein, the long-time editor of the *American Scholar* and a frequent contributor to the opinion pages of the *Wall Street Journal*. In a February 27, 2018, column, he acknowledged (metaphorically speaking) the elephant in the White House:

> I disapprove of the bragging tweets, the touchiness, the crude put-downs of anyone who disagrees with him ('Little Marco,' 'insecure Oprah,' 'Sloppy Steve,' and the rest), the unrestrained vulgarity. America has had ignorant, corrupt, vain, lazy presidents before, but in Donald Trump we have the first president who is a genuine boor. . . . Boors in their 70s do not change. Donald Trump is incorrigible. Not even John Kelly, a tough retired Marine Corps general, has been able to whip him into anything resembling presidential shape. With Mr. Trump, what we see is what we get, and what we get distinctly isn't Cary Grant.

Personality, however, is just one consideration. Policy is another, and in that regard the headline above Epstein's commentary speaks for him and like-minded Americans: "The Only Good Thing about Donald Trump Is All His Policies." Back during the Clinton presidency, analysts talked about the Arkansan's ability to compartmentalize: executive governing and worry about impeachment were kept in separate mental regions. In a way, for Trump's supporters, his personal behavior and his actions in office often demand from them a different kind of compartmentalization, one he would probably never recognize or really understand.

However, for many with experience in government and journalism, as well as for his partisan opponents, the president's verbal style is evidence of either a lack of basic knowledge or a willful effort to circulate untruths. In the spring of 2018, four experienced leaders in intelligence and security—Comey of the FBI; Michael Hayden, former director of the National Security Agency and Central Intelligence Agency; James Clapper, former director of National Intelligence; and John Brennan, head of the CIA from 2013 to 2017—went so far in books and articles as to accuse Trump of telling lies. Explaining his personal history with two Republican and two Democratic presidents, since George H. W. Bush in 1990, Brennan observed in a June 1, 2018, *Washington Post* commentary, "Presidents throughout the years have differed in their approaches to policy, based on political platforms, ideologies, and individual beliefs. Mr. Trump, however, has shown highly abnormal behavior by lying routinely to the American people without compunction, intentionally fueling divisions in our country and actively working to degrade the imperfect but critical institutions that serve us."

At the same time these veteran officials were leveling their criticism—Brennan's broadsides ultimately resulted in the president's revoking his security clearance in August 2018—Rex Tillerson, Trump's first secretary of state, who had been unceremoniously fired on Twitter, delivered a commencement address at Virginia Military Institute. Without naming anyone, Tillerson identified "a growing crisis in ethics and integrity" and went on to comment:

> If our leaders seek to conceal the truth or we as people become accepting of alternative realities that are no longer grounded in facts, then we as American citizens are on a

pathway to relinquishing our freedom. This is the life of nondemocratic societies comprised of people who are not free to seek the truth. We know them well. Societies in Russia, China, Iran, North Korea. You can complete the list. A responsibility of every American citizen to each other is to preserve and protect our freedom by recognizing what truth is and is not. What a fact is and is not. And begin by holding ourselves accountable through truthfulness and demand our pursuit of America's future be fact-based, not based on wishful thinking. Not hoped for outcomes made in shallow promises but with a clear-eyed view of the facts as they are and guided by the truth that will set us free to seek solutions to our most daunting challenges.

Tillerson's views are mainstream, traditional ones that are deeply rooted in the nation's democratic principles. A well-functioning democracy demands the constant flow of credible information so citizens can form judgments and opinions vital to self-governance. Yet if the truthfulness of a presidential announcement or pronouncement is doubtful or even untrustworthy, a prime question anyone should ask is a simple one: Why? More broadly, what motivates such linguistic behavior? What is the ultimate value of the citizenry's judgments and opinions if the information being considered is either inaccurate or fictitious?

To be fair and historically accurate, presidential devotion to unequivocal veracity is never listed as a distinguishing characteristic of White House occupants. In the years since World War II, Dwight Eisenhower denied there were U-2 spy planes flying over the Soviet Union, Lyndon Johnson claimed there had been an unprovoked attack in Vietnam's Gulf of Tonkin, Richard Nixon washed his hands of any Watergate involvement, Ronald Reagan vowed weapons weren't traded for hostages in Iran, Bill Clinton rebuffed charges of a sexual liaison with Monica Lewinsky, and George W. Bush asserted that Iraq possessed weapons of mass destruction—all statements of considerable consequence that proved to be untrue. What makes Trump stand out from previous presidents is the flagrancy and frequency with which he circulates misleading or untruthful information, either through speech or tweet. When nearly every utterance or observation is expressed in superlative or historic terms, it becomes difficult to calibrate factual accuracy. A president, who could be classified in charitable terms as "fabulist in chief," forces journalists and the public at large to approach what he says with a new set of political antennae.

Besides the contradictory or questionable statements, Trump's use of social media on occasion can—and does—propagate what could be classified as conspiracy theories. They seed doubts in the public's mind without surviving investigations of their authenticity or reliability, a habit he began before taking up residence at the White House—most notably with his unfounded assertion that Obama was born in Kenya rather than in the United States. Early in his presidency, Trump again went after Obama, tweeting out the claim that his predecessor in the Oval Office had bugged Trump Tower in New York. In less than a half hour on March 4, 2017, he sent these two exclamatory blasts to his followers and beyond: "Terrible! Just found out that Obama had my 'wires tapped' in Trump Tower just before the victory. Nothing found. This is McCarthyism!" and "How low has President Obama gone to tapp [sic] my phones during the very sacred election process. This is Nixon/Watergate. Bad (or sick) guy!" It's revelatory that earlier red-flag warnings of a "rigged election" were replaced with a solemn phrase suggesting just the opposite: "the very sacred election process." Much more importantly, however, the accusation was never substantiated.

A little over a year later, Trump returned to imputations about 2016 subterfuge, with, once again, parallels to Watergate featuring in his dramatization of the allegation. Insinuating that the FBI during Obama's last year in office inserted a clandestine mole in Trump's political organization, he tweeted on May 23, 2018, "SPYGATE could be one of the biggest political scandals in history!" By connecting the often-used suffix *gate*—a reliable linguistic marker of conspicuous wrongdoing and infamy—to the provocative word *spy*, Trump skillfully branded the putative conspiracy in an unforgettable way, and he kept driving this home for several days on Twitter and through statements to reporters. On June 6, he tweeted a quotation by a fellow believer in the deceit: "This makes the Nixon Watergate burglary look like keystone cop stuff." However, as with the wiretap assertion, no proof of a secret agent was revealed, and Republican leaders publicly stepped back from endorsing the president's cloak-and-dagger hypothesis. Yet even without evidence, Spygate persisted as a popular talking point for media favorable to Trump long after the allegation began to circulate. Whether a president will pay a political price for promoting unconfirmed broadsides is unknown. Interestingly, in most cases he's the victim or aggrieved party in the tall tale being told—the spoiling-for-a-fight attacker is now himself under attack. The dramatic shift brings a certain amount of sympathy, even if it is fleeting and unsubstantiated.

In his most unrestrained, uncompromising assault-and-insult mode, Trump took center stage during the 2018 midterm election season. "The Democratic Party is radical socialism—Venezuela—and open borders," he told rallies. "It is the party of crime, that is what it is." He also warned, "The Democrats have become too extreme. And they've become, frankly, too dangerous to govern. They've gone wacko. They want to destroy everything." Scare rhetoric, along with verbal rabbit punches directed at politicians from the opposing party, enlivened supporters at every Trump performance, and he didn't hold back: "In their lust for power, the Democrats have become totally unhinged. They've gone crazy." He even went so far as to engage in paradox: "I'm not on the ticket, but I am on the ticket. I want you to vote. Pretend I'm on the ballot."

When election officials started to count the votes cast, several senatorial and gubernatorial candidates Trump backed won their races; notably, Republicans were victorious over Democratic incumbents in Senate elections in Indiana, Missouri, and North Dakota. The GOP, in fact, extended their majority in the Senate from fifty-one to forty-nine to fifty-three to forty-seven. However, in the House of Representatives the Democrats flipped over three dozen seats to take control of that chamber by a margin of thirty-five districts: 235 to 200. The results nearly matched how well the party performed in the midterm after the most incriminating Watergate revelations and Richard Nixon's resignation in 1974. Indeed, in terms of total votes cast, Democrats exceeded the number they received post-Watergate, giving them 53.4 percent nationwide to the Republicans' 44.8 percent. And voter turnout reached 49.3 percent, the highest mark since 1914, when 50.4 percent of eligible voters went to the polls. Moreover, Democrats won seven governorships previously held by Republicans, including four in the Midwest: Illinois, Kansas, Michigan, and Wisconsin. (Trump won Kansas, Michigan, and Wisconsin in 2016.)

In a news conference the day after voters went to the polls, Trump said in opening remarks that "the Republican Party defied history to expand our Senate majority while significantly beating expectations in the House." Shortly thereafter, a reporter challenged the president's rosy appraisal: "You're a man who likes to win, but last night was not an absolute victory for you." Trump rejected the premise outright: "I'll be honest: I thought it was very close to complete victory. . . . I think it was a great victory. I'll be honest: I think it was a great victory. And, actually, some of the news this morning was that it was, in fact, a great victory."

Honestly, even if the midterms were either a nearly "complete" or just "a great" triumph, the president's public petulance in answering questions and in calling out by name eight losing Republican House incumbents who (in Trump's phrase) "didn't want the embrace" of his support suggested submerged pique, if not marinating anger. Not long after the ninety minutes of back-and-forth with journalists, the White House announced that Attorney General Jeff Sessions had been fired. The consequences of the midterm election were beginning to show, and other banishments from the administration became open secrets.

By November 18, less than two weeks after Election Day 2018, Trump began distancing himself from the vote tallies, telling Fox News, "I didn't run. I wasn't running. My name wasn't on the ballot. There are many people that think, 'I don't like Congress,' that like me a lot. I get it all the time: 'Sir, we'll never vote unless you're on the ballot.'" In the same interview, when he was asked to rank himself, the president said, "Look, I hate to do it, but I will do it, I would give myself an A+, is that enough? Can I go higher than that?"

That self-confident and superlative grade might be in jeopardy now that the Democrats have taken control of the House and begun to exercise their oversight authority and subpoena-charged capability to investigate the executive branch and its top officer. For example, the president's finances, including his long-concealed tax returns, are now fair game, along with any alleged scandal related to the 2016 campaign or his administration. When you think about it and take the longer view, for the first time since he became a business titan or a political figure, Trump is confronting a formal check on himself by an institution that has the power to scrutinize or probe questionable conduct, both private and public.

During his first two years in the Oval Office, Trump challenged the credibility of one institution after another: the intelligence community, the FBI, the "deep state," the news media, the judiciary, the Federal Reserve, the electoral process, and NATO, to name a few. Serving as president in the new political environment of divided government is a totally different experience for Trump; however, by the end of 2019, the federal government will have been divided for thirty-six of the fifty years since 1968, almost three-quarters of the time. Interestingly, Trump is the fourth consecutive president to suffer a significant midterm setback. A nation that is closely divided politically has found ways to keep the executive and at least one chamber of the legislative in the hands of different parties. By and large of late, voters have tended to prefer that powers be shared and checked, a reality that presidents, especially one like Trump, who has been conditioned to get his way, find frustrating to their governing agendas and personal situations.

With the unprecedented turnover of cabinet members and staff in this administration, there is the potential problem of insider criticism raising questions about the occupant of the Oval Office. For example, Omarosa Manigault Newman, who previously worked on Trump's reality-television show, released an unflattering memoir, *Unhinged* (2018), about her time as the White House director of communications for the Office of Public Liaison. In it, she accused the president of being "a racist, a bigot, and a misogynist," and of suffering from "mental decline." He fired back on Twitter that she, among other disparaging words, is "a lowlife." More probingly and substantively, Tillerson reflected on his tenure as secretary of state about nine months after leaving office. In a December 26, 2018, interview with CBS News' Bob Schieffer, the former Exxon Mobil chairman and chief executive commented, "It was challenging for me coming from the disciplined, highly process-oriented Exxon Mobil Corporation to go to work for a man who is pretty undisciplined, doesn't like to read, doesn't read briefing reports, doesn't like to get into the details of a lot of things, but rather just kind of says, 'Look, this is what I believe.'" He added that Trump would push for certain actions exceeding presidential authority: "So often, the president would say, 'Here's what I want to do, and here's how I want to do it.' And I would have to say to him, 'Mr. President, I understand what you want to do, but you can't do it that way. It violates the law. It violates the treaty.' He got really frustrated." Tillerson's revealing explanation of his foray into government service provoked a tweet from the person being described that declared the Texan was "dumb as a rock" and "lazy as hell." Derogatory reactions delivered through a so-called social medium are now to be expected, but they (in Tillerson's opinion) undermine democratic understanding and discourse: "I will be honest with you, it troubles me that the American people seem to want to know so little about issues, that they are satisfied with 128 characters." (Twitter actually allows users 140 or 280 characters—but the larger point deserves consideration.)

The first major confrontation to take place within the new actualities of the post-2016, midterm-election divided government erupted in the longest shutdown ever experienced by federal employees in the nation's history. The stumbling block, as far as the president was concerned, involved funding for a wall along the border between Mexico and the United States, which Trump had championed for three-and-a-half years. Though curiously little had been accomplished while Republicans controlled the executive and legislative branches in 2017 and 2018, the president forced the issue with Democrats, particularly House Speaker Nancy Pelosi and Senate minority leader Chuck Schumer. By 2019, the wall had become much more than a physical structure. It was now also an applause line-cum-crowd chant at Trump rallies and a potent political symbol that represented an elongated warning sign—DO NOT ENTER—for potential immigrants.

As a senator and as president, John Kennedy celebrated the contributions of new arrivals to America in two editions of his book *A Nation of Immigrants*. Trump's perspective reflected a decidedly different turn from Kennedy's approach. In fact, near the end of the speech announcing his candidacy in 2015—long after criticizing people from Mexico for bringing "lots of problems" to the United States—Trump boldly proclaimed, "I would build a great wall, and nobody builds walls better than me, believe me, and I'll build them very inexpensively. I will build a great, great wall on our southern border. And I will have Mexico pay for that wall. Mark my words."

Though the prepared remarks on the candidate's website never mentioned the source of payment, Trump kept marking his words, taking delight in repeating his promise and using it to excite, if not enrapture, his supporters. While Ronald Reagan invoked "the shining city upon a hill" in speech after speech,

Trump relied on the prospect of his "great, great wall" as a signature statement, the builder-businessman now speaking as the country's chief executive. The wall also appealed to many of the president's defenders—those "forgotten men and women"—worried or anxious about how new immigrants might change America in terms of employment opportunity, criminal activity, or demographic composition. All of Trump's talk about a wall contributed to the persona he was striving to project—a self-image of strength and toughness. When conservative commentator Ann Coulter titled one of her columns "Gutless President in Wall-less Country," Trump's resolve solidified, becoming, in its way, like concrete.

The government shutdown began on December 22, 2018, when Republicans still had majorities in both chambers of Congress, and lasted thirty-five days, until January 25, 2019, well after Democrats took control of the House. Jockeying for wall funding continued into Trump's third year in office, and grumbling on the right became something of a refrain. The president, however, kept assuring supporters by saying, "We're building the wall anyway."

Not satisfied with the $1.375 billion allocated for border fencing in a government-spending bill he signed on February 15, 2019, Trump decided to go around Congress by declaring a national emergency, a measure most often invoked to impose sanctions on foreign countries threatening US security. In this case, however, the president decided to take approximately $8 billion from the Pentagon and other departments to—in the new rallying cry of his supporters—"finish the wall." The action immediately provoked outrage on Capitol Hill and the filing of several lawsuits in federal courts. Announcing the national emergency, Trump said, "I could do the wall over a longer period of time. I didn't need to do this, but I'd rather do it much faster." The admission that he "didn't need to do this" struck observers as a perplexing way to describe an emergency.

Criticism or legal challenges of whatever origin and from whatever direction have never served as a deterrent to Trump's planning for the future. In fact, five hours after he was inaugurated in 2017, paperwork for his 2020 campaign was formally filed with the Federal Election Commission, the earliest submission of such documents in history. Two days before that, a reporter for the *Washington Post* revealed that Trump himself had already trademarked the slogan for his next campaign: "Keep America Great!" (complete with an exclamation point). Besides coming up with the motto and hiring a campaign manager, the president has already thought through what he expects to see happen in 2020. As with so much about him, the interpretation—published by the *New York Times* on December 28, 2017—both is personal and makes the speaker the focus of attention. "We're going to win another four years for a lot of reasons, most importantly because our country is starting to do well again and we're being respected again. But another reason that I'm going to win another four years is because newspapers, television, all forms of media will tank if I'm not there because without me, their ratings are going down the tubes. Without me, the *New York Times* will indeed be not the failing *New York Times*, but the failed *New York Times*. So they basically have to let me win. And eventually, probably six months before the election, they'll be loving me because they're saying, 'Please, please, don't lose Donald Trump.'"

Thirteen days later, on January 10, 2018, Trump (again using the third person to refer to himself) repeated his puzzling prognostication in remarks to his cabinet. The official White House transcript reports the president saying that "the media will ultimately support Trump in the end, because they're going to say, if Trump doesn't win in three years, they're all out of business."

The president's repulsion-attraction compulsion in approaching the mainstream media has developed into a hobby horse of his thinking, especially when he talks to journalists. Shortly after he participated in sessions at the United Nations in late September of 2018, he told a news conference that, in his opinion, the *New York Times* would support his reelection. He then elaborated, "I think ABC, CBS, NBC, the *Washington Post*, they're all going to endorse me, because if they don't they're all going out of business." What syndicated columnist George F. Will calls the president's "breezy indifference to reality" exists in several different realms.

If Donald Trump thinks the news media that he constantly lambastes on Twitter and elsewhere will recommend his reelection in 2020 for the sake of their financial survival, he must be hearing a voice, similar to the one Paul Ryan identified in 2016, that's inaudible to everybody else. An unconventional and unpredictable president produces a future of unknowable—and at times unbelievable—tomorrows. Let's assume, for the sake of argument, that the president will indeed seek the Republican nomination and a second term—though even speculating about the future in a book that is primarily historical in its substance challenges both common sense and literary classification.

Possibly the most important question to ask about 2020 is will "Trump fatigue" play a decisive role in the final outcome? How many voters will decide that continuing the daily White House drama another four years is too much to contemplate? There are signs already that the ever-spinning news cycle is whirling at such a rapid rate that people are signaling civic exhaustion or general queasiness. In the spring of 2018, the nonpartisan Pew Research Center released a study that reported 68 percent of those surveyed considered themselves worn out by the amount of news they were receiving. Just 30 percent "like the amount of news" to which they're exposed. The most fascinating finding of this research involves its politically partisan dimension. As the report notes, "Roughly three-quarters (77%) of Republicans and Republican-leaning independents feel worn out over how much news there is, compared with about six-in-ten Democrats and Democratic-leaning independents (61%)." Since coverage of the president and the Trump administration dominates so much of the news agenda, it's curious that Republicans feel a high level of fatigue. It's possible, however, that they consider much of the reporting overly negative in its treatment of Trump. In addition, the designation "Breaking News" flashes across television and computer screens so often during the Trump era that being constantly breathless in trying to keep up might not be an appealing prospect for Republicans, Democrats, or independents.

In mathematical vernacular, success in democratic politics usually comes from addition and multiplication rather than subtraction or division. From his inauguration through his first years in the White House, Trump has catered to his base of support with a fidelity and constancy that signal an attempt to deepen instead of broadening his core constituency. Viewed from this perspective, what we're seeing is a wedge presidency that puts a premium on issues that serve to divide, with the goal of expanding the numbers of like-minded supporters. Whether it's criticizing National Football League players for not standing during the national anthem, arguing that trade policies of previous presidents took advantage of American workers, or contending that illegal immigration is dangerously out of control, Trump makes little effort to (in the campaign slogan Nixon once used) "Bring Us Together." Is the Trump base broad enough to yield a winning bloc of voters in the necessary states for a second term? Will the multitude of investigations probing his business dealings, his (now-defunct) foundation, his campaign, his transition, his inauguration, and his administration result in specific charges that will lead to legal or governmental consequences, including even impeachment, removal from office, or resignation?

Possibly the most famous passage in Machiavelli's *The Prince* appears in chapter 17, when the question arises "whether it is better [for a prince] to be loved more than feared, or feared more than loved." Machiavelli answers with a diplomat's linguistic precision "that one ought to be both feared and loved, but as it is difficult for the two to go together, it is much safer to be feared than loved, if one of the two has to be wanting." Though Trump's grasp of political philosophy might be somewhat suspect, he did tell Bob Woodward and Robert Costa of the *Washington Post* before the 2016 election, "Real power is through respect. Real power is, I don't even want to use the word, fear."

In his book, *Fear: Trump in the White House* (2018), Woodward repeats the line "real power is fear" several times throughout the text. Like the emphasis on wedge-creating concerns, seeing the exercise of executive-branch power through the lens of fear sharpens those wedges, making a president less of a national father figure and more of a gruff, demanding boss. Can that approach work twice if there aren't public events along the way that feature a political figure's humane impulses and emotions? Americans want their president to fight fearlessly for them when it's necessary. But a constant state of combat or perpetual war can over time reduce the sense of fear inspired by a person trying to appear powerful. Moreover, demonizing every opponent as a long-term strategy for governance can ultimately backfire.

Since 2015, when he decided to participate in electoral politics, Donald Trump has played by his own rules, paying little attention to the established norms, traditions, and conventions. Sui generis certainly, he also exploited the existing system and current political tides—a chaotic nominating process, partisanship on steroids of vehemence, distrust of Washington's ways and means, the enticement of media celebrity, and all the rest—to win in 2016. Is his style and approach the future of politics in the United States? If so, what should be our national expectations for presidential leadership in the years ahead? The current moment should provoke more than these questions, as citizens—right, left, and broad center—try to draw lessons from a time that has taken all Americans into uncharted territory without the compass of history to guide their way to level and recognizable terrain.

—— EPILOGUE ——

The photo is of an ornate desk piled high with shakily stacked documents, while the text on the cover of the *Atlantic* features an article titled "How the Presidency Became Impossible." In smaller typeface, a reader learns, "It's Not Just Trump—the Job Is Now Too Much for Anyone." Spanning seventeen pages and nearly fourteen thousand words, the carefully reported essay by journalist and author John Dickerson, which appeared in May of 2018, is an exegesis of executive failure and frustration resulting from the job's "unfathomable psychological squeeze" and other exigencies.

A year earlier, Jeremi Suri, a professor of history at the University of Texas, published a learned yet accessible study *The Impossible Presidency: The Rise and Fall of America's Highest Office*, arguing that problems of governance are multiplying like lustful mice to the degree that electing a prime minister as well as a president "at different intervals" would help shift some leadership responsibilities to another person. "A single executive for an enterprise as gargantuan and labyrinthine as the United States has become anachronistic," Suri asserts near the end of his analysis (293).

The impossibility of the presidency is a recurring theme that's as old as the republic. The first occupants of the office put their own gloomy anxiety about the position they devised in words. In his first inaugural address, George Washington fretted about "the magnitude and difficulty of the trust," and, of course, Thomas Jefferson was poetically paradoxical by recognizing the "splendid misery" of White House leadership. However, to call the presidency an impossible job is more than anything exasperated exaggeration, a figure of speech rather than a well-tempered judgment. Without question, it is difficult and demanding—but it is not impossible.

Of course, the growth in the executive branch, along with the expansion of America's role in the world and concomitant threats and dangers, contributed much greater complexity to the nation's preeminent political position since the founders' years. But a radically changed reality doesn't mean that the office itself should fundamentally change. Certainly, the nominating process for presidential candidates deserves thoughtful reform, and the Twenty-Second Amendment, with its imposition of arbitrary, temporal limitations on executive authority and power, warrants repeal. And extracting some of the poisonous partisanship from the body politic would decrease the polarization and definitely help relations between the White House and Capitol Hill.

The search for the most capable successors to Washington or Jefferson—or Lincoln or either Roosevelt—begins with us. Voters need to evaluate aspirants to this unique job more diligently and thoroughly before casting their ballots every four years. Except for my-party-right-or-wrong Democrats or Republicans, the choice is rarely easy, because so many considerations come into play to pick one nakedly ambitious yet humanly fallible person.

Civics books provide standardized discussions of a president's different roles. A lone officeholder simultaneously juggles service as head of state, head of government, commander in chief, dominant diplomat, principal policy initiator, and party head. In more recent years, presidents have also assumed unofficial assignments indispensable to their work: consoler in chief (at national tragedies and disasters), celebrity in chief (at special events on behalf of the country), and cheerleader in chief (in promoting the economy and American values). Because of the office's expanding range of duties and responsibilities, a president's collection of hats related to work rivals what one sees among women attending the Kentucky Derby. Nobody can possess, in equal measure, the skills of a leader, an administrator, a commander, a negotiator, an educator, a pastor, and an actor. But the talents of those vocations (and others) are required of anyone wanting to labor and to live at 1600 Pennsylvania Avenue today.

Though possibly not central to every role, power and its exercise animate what a president does from a day's first moments until its last. Ambition fuels the drive, but power is its final destination. How someone might handle power and its responsibilities should be a voter's prime concern; however, it's often impossible to know what a nation's leader will do in certain circumstances or specific situations. In *The Passage to Power*, volume 4 of Robert A. Caro's monumental biography *The Years of Lyndon Johnson*, Caro devotes a portion of the introduction to a discussion of power and how Johnson saw it at the beginning of his presidency, a few days after the Kennedy assassination. The passage is worth quoting at length:

> But although the cliché says that power always corrupts, what is seldom said, but what is equally true, is that power always *reveals*. When a man is climbing, trying to persuade others to give him power, concealment is necessary: to hide traits that might make others reluctant to give him power, to hide also what he wants to do with that power; if men recognized the traits or realized the aims, they might refuse to give him what he wants. But as a man obtains more power, camouflage is less necessary. The curtain begins to rise. The revealing begins. When Lyndon Johnson had accumulated

enough power to do something—a small something—for civil rights in the Senate, he had done it, inadequate though it may have been. Now, suddenly, he had a lot more power, and it didn't take him long to reveal at least part of what he wanted to do with it. On the evening of November 26, the advisers gathered around the dining room in his home to draft the speech he was to deliver the following day to a joint session of Congress were arguing about the amount of emphasis to be given to civil rights in that speech, his first major address as President. As Johnson sat silently listening, most of these advisers were warning that he must not emphasize the subject because it would antagonize the southerners who controlled Congress, and whose support he would need for the rest of his presidency—and because a civil rights bill had no chance of passage anyway. And then, in the early hours of the morning, as one of those advisers recalls, "one of those wise, practical people around the table" told him to his face that a President shouldn't spend his time and power on lost causes, no matter how worthy those causes might be. "Well, what the hell's the presidency for?" Lyndon Johnson replied. (xiv–xv)

Johnson signed the Civil Rights Act into law six months later on July 2. The following summer he signed the Voting Rights Act of 1965. Each time, Johnson's signature answered his question about what the presidency is for, and the purpose of his power became unmistakable to American eyes.

How can a citizen evaluate the exercise of power? History can help provide some direction. In *The Presidential Difference* (2000), Fred I. Greenstein analyzes the leadership style and performance of White House occupants since Franklin Roosevelt. He identifies six qualities he considers critical in evaluating someone in the highest office: "effectiveness as a public communicator," "organizational capacity," "political skill," "vision," "cognitive style," and "emotional intelligence." And the greatest of these, in Greenstein's judgment, is emotional intelligence—

the ability to be emotionally aware of yourself and others and to manage emotions in the most appropriate and successful way. "Beware the presidential contender who lacks emotional intelligence," he observes. "In its absence all else may turn to ashes" (200).

Greenstein's discriminating qualities come into sharper focus with hindsight after four or eight years, when it's possible to review an administration's entire record. But what should we take into account *before* voting on Election Day every four years? After decades of teaching about the American presidency, I developed an informal checklist of concerns that a student-citizen could research on her or his own before making a decision. Investigating each concern necessitates assessing a variety of sources provided by both the candidates and the media, as they (in all of their contemporary abundance) present reporting, analysis, and commentary.

> *Credibility*—Is a candidate making statements on the basis of accurate information so that an argument on behalf of a policy proposal has a strong, reliable foundation on which to build a government initiative or program?
>
> *Character*—Is a candidate's biography a reflection of the life and work of someone who merits civic trust and confidence on judgments affecting life and death matters for the United States and the world?
>
> *Courage/Conviction*—Is a candidate of sufficient strength of spine to make difficult decisions and to see them either to their conclusion or to their modification, should serious problems arise?
>
> *Curiosity*—Is a candidate inquisitive enough about other peoples, cultures, programs, and history such that due diligence, and due intelligence, is performed when addressing complicated problems?
>
> *Creativity*—Is a candidate able to address and evaluate a dilemma or dispute innovatively, demonstrating an ability to think and act without the restrictions that might come from an existing framework in need of new appraisal?

Choosing a president takes time, which is one reason why the nominating process and the general election encompass so many months in the United States. Occupants of the White House might consider the office "a glorious burden," but ordinary voters quadrennially face a glorious guessing game. Who measures up to the obligations and requirements thrust on the nation's leader? Who possesses the talent and temperament for the job? Who can inspire millions of other people to take action that might be difficult or even unpopular?

One of America's most acute observers during the twentieth century was author and academic Max Lerner, who wrote a classic—and mammoth—study of this country's unique nationhood in all its distinctiveness and variety, *America as a Civilization* (1957). "Our destiny as a people rests not in our stars but in ourselves," Lerner remarked in a widely circulated essay for *Newsweek* that appeared on October 8, 1979. "I am neither optimist nor pessimist. I am a possibilist" (21). The presidency is not impossible. It is an office of the possible for rare individuals able to master the relentless responsibilities of executive governance at the center, both vital and unique, of America's democratic republic.

A CHRONOLOGY OF THE MODERN AMERICAN PRESIDENCY

March 21, 1947   The Eightieth Congress (and the first since the Seventy-First from 1929 to 1931 to have Republican majorities in both the House of Representatives and the Senate) approves a joint resolution proposing a constitutional amendment that states a person may not be elected president more than twice. The proposed amendment was drafted and passed less than two years after Franklin Roosevelt's death on April 12, 1945.

November 2, 1948   Harry Truman is elected president over two-time Republican candidate Thomas E. Dewey, the governor of New York. Strom Thurmond, the governor of South Carolina and the nominee of the States' Rights Democratic Party (the "Dixiecrats") and former vice president Henry Wallace, the Progressive Party candidate, also draw nearly 5 percent of the popular vote between them.

February 27, 1951	The Twenty-Second Amendment to the Constitution limiting a president to two terms is ratified by the requisite number of states, or thirty-six of the forty-eight that had been admitted.
September 23, 1952	Republican vice-presidential candidate Richard Nixon delivers his "Checkers" speech on national television, denying any impropriety related to the use of money coming from political supporters.
November 4, 1952	Dwight D. Eisenhower defeats Illinois governor Adlai Stevenson for president and becomes the first Republican to win the White House since Herbert Hoover in 1928.
December 8, 1954	At the United Nations, Eisenhower delivers his "Atoms for Peace" proposal.
November 6, 1956	Eisenhower is reelected president, beating Stevenson for a second time and by a wider margin than in 1952.
September 9, 1957	Eisenhower signs into law the Civil Rights Act of 1957, establishing the Civil Rights Division in the Justice Department and creating the Civil Rights Commission.
September 24, 1958	Eisenhower orders federal troops to Little Rock, Arkansas, to help with the desegregation of public schools there.
October 7, 1958	Eisenhower's long-time chief of staff, Sherman Adams, is forced to resign for accepting expensive gifts in a scandal that tarnished the administration during its second term.

May 1, 1960	An American U-2 reconnaissance plane is shot down while flying in airspace of the Soviet Union. The State Department initially denies intelligence gathering was taking place but quickly ends the attempt to cover up the spying. Eisenhower's June visit to the Soviet Union is cancelled.
September 26, 1960	Senator John Kennedy and Vice President Nixon engage in the first of four televised presidential debates, each drawing more than sixty million viewers.
November 8, 1960	Kennedy defeats Nixon by a little more than a hundred thousand votes of over sixty-eight million cast.
January 17, 1961	In his farewell address as president, Eisenhower says that "we must guard against the acquisition of unwarranted influence, whether sought or unsought, by the military-industrial complex."
April 13, 1961	In Berlin, construction begins of a wall that prevents residents of East Germany from entering West Germany.
October 28, 1962	The thirteen-day Cuban Missile Crisis between the Soviet Union and the United States ends with the Soviets and Americans agreeing to remove their missiles from, respectively, Cuba and Turkey.
November 22, 1963	Kennedy is assassinated in Dallas, Texas, and Lyndon Johnson is sworn in as the thirty-sixth president.

July 2, 1964	Johnson signs into law the Civil Rights Act of 1964 and reportedly tells an assistant that the legislation will result in southern Democrats switching their allegiances to the Republican Party.
August 7, 1964	The Gulf of Tonkin resolution, formalizing and deepening US involvement in the Vietnam War, is passed by Congress.
November 3, 1964	Johnson wins a full term as president, losing just five southern states and the home state (Arizona) of his opponent, Senator Barry Goldwater.
July 30, 1965	Johnson signs amendments to the Social Security Act that create Medicare and Medicaid as national health insurance programs for older and less fortunate Americans.
February 10, 1967	The Twenty-Fifth Amendment addressing presidential succession and disability is ratified, and—for the first time—a vacancy in the vice presidency can be filled when the president's nominee is confirmed by majority votes in the House and the Senate.
March 16, 1968	Senator Robert Kennedy declares his candidacy for the Democratic presidential nomination. On June 6, after winning the California primary, he dies from an assassin's bullet in Los Angeles.
March 31, 1968	At the end of a speech to the nation proposing peace talks and a partial halt to the bombing of North Vietnam, Johnson says he will not seek reelection in that year's campaign.

April 4, 1968	Reverend Martin Luther King Jr. is assassinated in Memphis, Tennessee, sparking riots in many American cities.
April 27, 1968	Vice President Hubert Humphrey announces he will pursue the Democratic nomination for president and concentrates on collecting delegates in states where party leaders, rather than primary voters, are influential.
August 29, 1968	Without competing in any primaries, Humphrey is nominated to be his party's standard-bearer during a national convention in Chicago that is marred by violence and later called a "police riot."
November 5, 1968	Nixon returns the White House to the GOP after eight years of Democratic occupancy, defeating Humphrey and George Wallace of the American Independent Party, who carries five southern states.
February 8, 1969	The Democratic Party creates the Commission on Party Structure and Delegate Selection, known subsequently as the McGovern-Fraser Commission, to reform the delegate-selection process. On November 19–20, 1969, the commission adopts official guidelines for delegate selection, which opens up the process.
July 1, 1971	The Twenty-Sixth Amendment to the Constitution, lowering the voting age from twenty-one to eighteen, is ratified.
February 21, 1972	Nixon arrives in the People's Republic of China, opening the door for diplomatic relations with the world's most populous Communist country.

June 17, 1972	Five men connected to Nixon's reelection effort are arrested after they break into the offices of the Democratic National Committee located in the Watergate complex in Washington, DC.
November 7, 1972	Nixon trounces Senator George McGovern in both the popular vote and the Electoral College to secure a second term. It is the fifth time in the last six presidential elections that Nixon has been on the ballot as either the Republican standard-bearer or as the vice-presidential candidate.
October 10, 1973	Spiro Agnew resigns as vice president for accepting money illegally while a public official. He pleads no contest to a felony charge of tax evasion.
December 6, 1973	House Minority Leader Gerald Ford is confirmed as vice president, receiving 92 yes (and 3 no) votes in the Senate and 387 yes (and 35 no) votes in the House.
July 27–30, 1974	Over a three-day period, the House Judiciary Committee approves three articles of impeachment against Nixon, but the full House never conducts a vote on the articles.
August 9, 1974	Nixon resigns as president, and Vice President Ford takes the oath of office, saying in his formal remarks that "our long national nightmare is over."
September 8, 1974	Ford pardons Nixon for "all offenses against the United States" during Nixon's time as president.

January 19, 1976	In the Democratic Party caucuses for president in Iowa, the designation "uncommitted" receives 37 percent of the vote, followed by former Georgia governor Jimmy Carter with 27 percent. Carter takes advantage of the media attention to catapult to the lead over several other candidates. In the Republican Party's caucuses, Ford defeats former California governor Ronald Reagan 45 to 43 percent, beginning a seesaw race for the White House nomination.
August 18, 1976	Ford receives 1,187 delegate votes to Reagan's 1,070 and becomes the Republican nominee at the party's national convention.
September 23, 1976	Ford and Carter debate, the first such face-off between presidential candidates since 1960 and the beginning of televised debates as a regular feature of national elections. Ford also becomes the first incumbent president ever to debate a challenger.
November 2, 1976	Carter wins the presidential election against Ford, who becomes the first former president and former vice president to serve in the two national offices without being elected to either.
September 17, 1978	At a White House ceremony, after twelve days of negotiations, Israeli prime minister Menachem Begin and Egyptian president Anwar Sadat sign the Camp David Accords, which were negotiated with Carter's participation. On March 26, 1979, again at the White House, Begin and Sadat sign a peace treaty between their two countries.

November 4, 1979	Supporters of the Iranian Revolution take sixty-six Americans hostages in Tehran, fifty-two of whom remain in custody for 444 days—until Carter's term as president ends on January 20, 1981.
April 24, 1980	A US military operation to rescue the hostages in Iran fails and results in the death of eight American soldiers.
May 20, 1980	Reagan clinches the GOP presidential nomination by amassing more delegates than chief rivals George H. W. Bush and Congressman John Anderson.
August 14, 1980	Carter is renominated by Democrats to head the national ticket after overcoming a challenge from Senator Edward Kennedy in the primaries and caucuses.
November 4, 1980	Reagan soundly defeats Carter, the second consecutive incumbent president to lose the office in an election.
March 30, 1981	Reagan is seriously wounded in an assassination attempt in Washington, DC, and hospitalized almost two weeks before returning to the White House for the remainder of his recovery. On April 28, 1981, he delivers a speech to a joint session of Congress, his first since being shot.
March 23, 1983	Reagan proposes the Strategic Defense Initiative, popularly referred to as "Star Wars," to counter the threat of ballistic missiles fired by the Soviet Union, which Reagan had called "an evil empire" on March 8, 1983.

November 6, 1984	Reagan wins a second term by beating former vice president Walter Mondale, who carried just his home state of Minnesota and the District of Columbia.
November 3, 1986	The trading of arms to Iran in exchange for hostages, with the profits sent to the Contras in Nicaragua, becomes known through news reports and is referred to as the Iran-Contra affair or scandal.
February 19, 1987	The Commission on Presidential Debates, an independent organization committed to ensuring debates take place before national elections, is formally established.
March 4, 1987	From the Oval Office, Reagan tells the nation, "A few months ago I told the American people I did not trade arms for hostages. My heart and my best intentions still tell me that's true, but the facts and evidence tell me it is not." Revelations of the Iran-Contra affair result in a precipitous decline in Reagan's approval rating throughout 1987 before it rebounds in 1988.
April 13, 1987	Former senator Gary Hart announces his candidacy for the Democratic Party's presidential nomination. However, stories about alleged marital infidelity that appear in early May lead to his withdrawing from the campaign on May 8, 1987.
July 1, 1987	Reagan nominates US Appeals Court judge Robert Bork to be an associate justice of the Supreme Court. The Senate rejects Bork's nomination fifty-eight to forty-two on Octo-

ber 23, 1987, with two Democrats supporting him and six Republicans voting against him.

November 8, 1988   George H. W. Bush becomes the first sitting vice president since Martin Van Buren (1836) to win the White House.

November 9, 1989   The Berlin Wall, one of the most recognizable symbols of the Cold War between Western democracy and Soviet Communism, begins to come down.

January 16, 1991   G. H. W. Bush announces the beginning of Operation Desert Storm to drive Iraqi occupying forces from Kuwait. The US-led coalition concludes hostilities victoriously on February 28, 1991, with Iraq recognizing the sovereignty of Kuwait. Gallup measures Bush's approval rating at 89 percent that February.

February 1, 1992   Bush and Russian president Boris Yeltsin declare a formal end to the Cold War and sign a declaration that says, "Russia and the United States do not regard each other as potential adversaries."

November 3, 1992   G. H. W. Bush becomes the third incumbent president since 1976 to lose an election, as Arkansas governor Bill Clinton, a Democrat, wins against both Bush and Ross Perot, an independent candidate who receives nearly twenty million votes.

December 8, 1993   Clinton signs the North American Free Trade Agreement (NAFTA) into law, after Republicans supported the legislation in greater numbers than Democrats in both the House of Representatives and the Senate.

May 6, 1994	Paula Corbin Jones, a former Arkansas state employee, files a sexual harassment lawsuit against Clinton.
November 8, 1994	In the first special and midterm elections of the Clinton presidency, the Democrats lose fifty-four House and eight Senate seats, giving the Republicans a two-chamber majority in Congress for the first time since 1953.
November 5, 1996	Clinton retains the White House but, for the second time, he is denied a majority of popular votes because of the support received by two other candidates: former GOP senator Bob Dole and Ross Perot, now of the Reform Party.
January 17, 1998	The Drudge Report posts an item that *Newsweek* spiked a story about a possible affair between President Clinton and a former White House intern.
January 21, 1998	The *Washington Post* and other news organizations report the name of Monica Lewinsky, the former intern, and the possibility of a sexual relationship between her and Clinton.
April 10, 1998	The Good Friday Agreement to establish a power-sharing agreement in Northern Ireland is signed after Clinton invests his time and influence to help end the three-decade-long sectarian conflict called "the Troubles."
August 17, 1998	In an address to the nation from the White House, Clinton admits to having had "an inappropriate relationship" with Lewinsky but denies "unlawful action."

November 13, 1998 — Clinton agrees to pay Jones $850,000 to settle the harassment lawsuit against him.

December 19, 1998 — Clinton is impeached by the House of Representatives on charges of perjury and obstruction of justice. On February 12, 1999, the Senate acquits him of both charges.

December 18, 2000 — Voting by members of the Electoral College in each state declares Texas governor George W. Bush the president after the Supreme Court on December 12 rules five to four to stop the recount of ballots in contested Florida counties. Though Clinton's vice president, Al Gore, receives more popular votes nationwide, Bush secures 271 electors, one more than the required number.

June 7, 2001 — Bush signs the Economic Growth and Tax Relief Reconciliation Act, the first major piece of legislation of his presidency, which mandates a $1.35 trillion tax cut between 2001 and 2011.

September 11, 2001 — Terrorists using hijacked airplanes kill nearly three thousand people in New York, Washington, DC, and Pennsylvania. The attacks initiate what becomes known as the "War on Terror," resulting in massive governmental changes.

October 7, 2001 — The US military response to the 9/11 attacks begins with a series of strikes on terrorist-training camps in Afghanistan.

November 25, 2002 — The Homeland Security Act, signed into law by Bush, establishes the US Department of Homeland Security.

March 20, 2003	A "shock-and-awe" bombing campaign launches the Iraq War to overthrow the country's dictator, Saddam Hussein, and his government. US troops fight in Iraq until December 18, 2011.
May 1, 2003	Standing in front of a sign announcing "Mission Accomplished" on the aircraft carrier *USS Abraham Lincoln*, Bush declares that major combat operations in Iraq are complete.
November 2, 2004	Bush wins a second term with his victory over Massachusetts senator John Kerry in the only election between 1992 and 2016 when a Republican received the most popular votes.
August 29, 2005	Hurricane Katrina strikes the US Gulf Coast, causing an estimated hundred billion dollars in damage across Louisiana, Mississippi, and Alabama. Criticism of the Bush administration's response leads to a pronounced decline in the president's approval ratings, with his second-term average being 37 percent, according to Gallup.
November 7, 2006	Bush's declining popularity and the protracted combat in Iraq help Democrats take control of both the House and the Senate in the midterm elections.
June 3, 2008	After a nominating process that begins on January 3 with the Iowa caucuses, Senator Barack Obama secures enough delegates to win the Democratic presidential nomination over Senator Hillary Clinton.

September 24, 2008	Bush tells the nation, "We're in the midst of a serious financial crisis," and that crisis becomes known as "the Great Recession." In October 2008, Bush's approval rating plunges to 25 percent, according to Gallup, the lowest of his presidency.
November 4, 2008	Obama, who is of African American heritage, becomes the first member of a minority to win the presidency and the first senator since Kennedy to move directly to the White House from Congress.
March 23, 2010	Obama signs into law the Patient Protection and Affordable Care Act, popularly known as "Obamacare," which receives no Republican support in either the House or the Senate.
November 2, 2010	Democrats drop sixty-three House and six Senate seats in the midterm elections, relinquishing their majority in the House.
March 17, 2011	Real estate developer and television performer Donald J. Trump tells ABC's *Good Morning America* that he doubts whether Obama was born in the United States, saying, "It's very strange. The whole thing is very strange."
April 27, 2011	The White House releases Obama's birth certificate that states he was born in Honolulu, Hawaii, on August 4, 1961.
November 6, 2012	Obama is reelected over former Massachusetts governor Mitt Romney, becoming the third consecutive two-term president. The only other time in US history when such a streak occurred was at the beginning of the

nineteenth century (from 1801 to 1825) with the two-term presidencies of Thomas Jefferson, James Madison, and James Monroe.

October 1, 2013 — The governmental website for enrolling in Obamacare launches but repeatedly crashes, provoking broad criticism of Obama and his administration.

November 4, 2014 — The second midterm elections of the Obama presidency result in Democratic losses of thirteen more House seats and nine in the Senate, leading to Republican control of both chambers of Congress.

December 12, 2015 — Obama announces the approval in France of the US-backed Paris Climate Agreement to lower greenhouse gas emissions.

November 8, 2016 — Though behind in the popular vote count by nearly three million ballots, Republican Donald Trump achieves an Electoral College victory over Hillary Clinton, while the GOP retains congressional majorities.

May 9, 2017 — Trump fires James Comey, director of the Federal Bureau of Investigation, and later states in a television interview that the Justice Department's inquiry into alleged Russian involvement in his 2016 election was a reason for the action.

June 1, 2017 — Trump announces that the United States will withdraw from the 2015 Paris Climate Agreement.

December 22, 2017 — Trump signs the Tax Cuts and Jobs Act, which many analysts consider the most significant tax-code overhaul in three decades and which it is estimated will increase the government's budget deficit by $1.5 trillion over the next ten years.

March 13, 2018   Trump uses his Twitter account to dismiss Rex Tillerson as secretary of state.

May 8, 2018   Trump announces that the United States is withdrawing from the Iranian nuclear deal, formally known as the Joint Comprehensive Plan of Action.

June 12, 2018   After calling North Korea's supreme leader, Kim Jong Un, "Rocket Man" in a speech at the United Nations, Trump meets with Kim in Singapore to discuss denuclearization of North Korea.

July 16, 2018   Trump and Russian president Vladimir Putin engage in a summit in Helsinki, which is followed by a news conference that includes Trump's reacting to questions about whether Russia meddled during the 2016 presidential campaign.

November 6, 2018   In the 2018 midterm elections, Democrats increase their total number of seats in the House of Representatives from 193 to 235 to take control of the chamber in 2019 (for the first time since early 2011), while Republicans strengthen their majority in the Senate by picking up two additional seats for a 53 to 47 majority.

FOR FURTHER READING

This highly selective bibliography includes but is not limited to all works quoted or referred to in the text. It does *not* include biographies or studies of individual presidents—indispensable resources for understanding the office at a particular time and the institution in its broader historical context—unless they are actually cited.

Bai, Matt. *All the Truth Is Out: The Week Politics Went Tabloid*. New York: Alfred A. Knopf, 2014.

Beschloss, Michael R. *Presidential Courage: Brave Leaders and How They Changed America, 1789–1989*. New York: Simon and Schuster, 2007.

Brokaw, Tom. *The Greatest Generation*. New York: Random House, 1998.

Brownstein, Ronald. *The Second Civil War: How Extreme Partisanship Has Paralyzed Washington and Polarized America*. New York: Penguin, 2007.

Burnham, Walter Dean. *The Current Crisis in American Politics*. New York: Oxford University Press, 1982.

Burns, James MacGregor. *The Power to Lead: The Crisis of the American Presidency*. New York: Simon and Schuster, 1984.

———. *Presidential Government: The Crucible of Leadership*. Boston: Houghton Mifflin, 1966.

Caro, Robert. *The Passage of Power.* Vol. 4 of *The Years of Lyndon Johnson.* New York: Alfred A. Knopf, 2012.

Chua, Amy. *Political Tribes: Group Instinct and the Fate of Nations.* New York: Penguin Press, 2018.

Cohen, Marty, David Karol, Hans Noel, and John Zaller. *The Party Decides: Presidential Nominations before and after Reform.* Chicago: University of Chicago Press, 2008.

Cronin, Thomas E., and Michael A. Genovese. *The Paradoxes of the American Presidency.* New York: Oxford University Press, 1998.

Cunliffe, Marcus. *The Presidency.* 3rd ed. Boston: Houghton Mifflin, 1987.

Dallek, Robert. *Hail to the Chief: The Making and Unmaking of American Presidents.* New York: Hyperion, 1996.

Dionne, E. J. Jr. *Why Americans Hate Politics.* New York: Simon and Schuster, 1991.

Donald, David Herbert. *Lincoln.* New York: Simon and Schuster, 1995.

Gibbs, Nancy, and Michael Duffy. *The Presidents Club: Inside the World's Most Exclusive Fraternity.* New York: Simon and Schuster, 2012.

Gingrich, Newt. *Lessons Learned the Hard Way: A Personal Report.* New York: HarperCollins, 1998.

Goodwin, Doris Kearns. *Leadership in Turbulent Times.* New York: Simon and Schuster, 2018.

Greenberg, David. *Republic of Spin: An Inside History of the American Presidency.* New York: W. W. Norton, 2016.

Greenstein, Fred I. *The Presidential Difference: Leadership Style from FDR to Clinton.* New York: Free Press, 2000.

Hamilton, Nigel. *American Caesars: Lives of the Presidents from Franklin D. Roosevelt to George W. Bush.* New Haven, CT: Yale University Press, 2010.

Hess, Stephen. *Presidents and the Presidency.* Washington, DC: Brookings Institution, 1996.

Howell, William G. *Thinking about the Presidency: The Primacy of Power.* With David Milton Brent. Princeton, NJ: Princeton University Press, 2013.

Hughes, Emmet John. *The Living Presidency: The Resources and Dilemmas of the American Presidential Office.* New York: Coward, McCann and Geoghegan, 1973.

Jamieson, Kathleen Hall. *Packaging the Presidency: A History and Criticism of Presidential Campaign Advertising.* New York: Oxford University Press, 1984.

Kalb, Marvin. *Enemy of the People: Trump's War on the Press, the New McCarthyism, and the Threat to American Democracy.* Washington, DC: Brookings Institution Press, 2018.

Kamarck, Elaine C. *Why Presidents Fail: And How They Can Succeed Again.* Washington, DC: Brookings Institution Press, 2016.

Kernell, Samuel. *Going Public: New Strategies of Presidential Leadership.* Washington, DC: CQ Press, 1986.

Kessler, Ronald. *The Trump White House: Changing the Rules of the Game.* New York: Crown Forum, 2018.

Langston, Thomas S. *With Reverence and Contempt: How Americans Think about Their President.* Baltimore: Johns Hopkins University Press, 1995.

Laski, Harold. *The American Presidency.* New York: Harper and Brothers, 1940.

Lerner, Max. *America as a Civilization: Life and Thought in the United States Today.* New York: Simon and Schuster, 1957.

———. *Wounded Titans: American Presidents and the Perils of Power.* Edited by Robert Schmuhl. New York: Arcade, 1996.

Leuchtenburg, William E. *The American President: From Teddy Roosevelt to Bill Clinton.* New York: Oxford University Press, 2015.

Lowi, Theodore J. *The End of Liberalism: The Second Republic of the United States.* 2nd ed. New York: W. W. Norton, 1979.

Mackenzie, G. Calvin. *The Imperiled Presidency: Leadership Challenges in the Twenty-First Century.* Lanham, MD: Rowman and Littlefield, 2017.

Mayer, William G., ed. *In Pursuit of the White House: How We Choose Our Presidential Nominees.* Chatham, NJ: Chatham House, 1996.

McDonald, Forrest. *The American Presidency: An Intellectual History.* Lawrence: University Press of Kansas, 1994.

Miller, Aaron David. *End of Greatness: Why America Can't Have (and Doesn't Want) Another Great President*. New York: Palgrave Macmillan, 2014.

Minow, Newton N., and Craig L. Lamay. *Inside the Presidential Debates: Their Improbable Past and Promising Future*. Chicago: University of Chicago Press, 2008.

Neustadt, Richard E. *Presidential Power and the Modern Presidents: The Politics of Leadership from Roosevelt to Reagan*. New York: Free Press, 1990.

———. *Presidential Power: The Politics of Leadership*. New York: John Wiley and Sons, 1960.

Polsby, Nelson W. *Consequences of Party Reform*. New York: Oxford University Press, 1983.

Reedy, George E. *The Twilight of the Presidency: From Johnson to Reagan*. Rev. ed. New York: New American Library, 1987.

Reeves, Richard. *President Kennedy: Profile of Power*. New York: Simon and Schuster, 1993.

Rosenberg, Howard, and Charles S. Feldman. *No Time to Think: The Menace of Media Speed and the 24-Hour News Cycle*. New York: Continuum, 2008.

Rossiter, Clinton. *The American Presidency*. 2nd ed. New York: Harcourt, Brace, 1960.

Safire, William. *Safire's Political Dictionary*. Rev. ed. New York: Oxford University Press, 2008.

Schlesinger, Arthur M. Jr. *The Imperial Presidency*. Boston: Houghton Mifflin, 1973.

———. *War and the American Presidency*. New York: W. W. Norton, 2004.

Schmuhl, Robert. *Statecraft and Stagecraft: American Political Life in the Age of Personality*. 2nd ed. Notre Dame, IN: University of Notre Dame Press, 1992.

Shogan, Robert. *The Double-Edged Sword: How Character Makes and Ruins Presidents, from Washington to Clinton*. Boulder, CO: Westview Press, 1999.

———. *None of the Above: Why Presidents Fail—And What Can Be Done about It*. New York: New American Library, 1982.

———. *The Riddle of Power: Presidential Leadership from Truman to Bush*. New York: Dutton, 1991.

Skowronek, Stephen. *The Politics Presidents Make: Leadership from John Adams to Bill Clinton*. Cambridge, MA: Belknap Press of Harvard University Press, 1997.

Suri, Jeremi. *The Impossible Presidency: The Rise and Fall of America's Highest Office*. New York: Basic Books, 2017.

Taranto, James, and Leonard Leo, eds. *Presidential Leadership: Rating the Best and the Worst in the White House*. New York: Wall Street Journal/Free Press, 2004.

Tocqueville, Alexis de. *Democracy in America*. Edited by J. P. Mayer and Max Lerner. Translated by George Lawrence. New York: Harper and Row, 1966.

Truman, Harry S. *Mr. Citizen*. New York: Bernard Geis, 1960.

Trump, Donald J. *Trump: The Art of the Deal*. With Tony Schwartz. New York: Ballantine Books, 2005. First published 1987 by Random House.

Tulis, Jeffrey. *The Rhetorical Presidency*. Princeton, NJ: Princeton University Press, 1987.

White, Theodore H. *America in Search of Itself: The Making of the President 1956–1980*. New York: Harper and Row, 1982.

Wilson, Robert A., ed. *Character above All: The Presidents from FDR to George Bush*. New York: Simon and Schuster, 1995.

———. *Power and the Presidency*. New York: PublicAffairs, 1999.

Wolff, Michael. *Fire and Fury: Inside the Trump White House*. New York: Henry Holt, 2018.

Woodward, Bob. *Fear: Trump in the White House*. New York: Simon and Schuster, 2018

———. *Shadow: Five Presidents and the Legacy of Watergate*. New York: Simon and Schuster, 1999.

ACKNOWLEDGMENTS

In the prologue, I confessed to a lifetime of White House watching. Since the 1970s, I've written scores of journal articles, magazine essays, newspaper or online columns, and lectures about the American presidency and individual presidents. Not long after the 2016 campaign, which challenged so many customs and conventions, I approached Stephen M. Wrinn, the director of the University of Notre Dame Press, about the possibility of a volume collecting several previously published disquisitions on presidential subjects. Steve reacted by asking a question that also delivered a suggestion: What about a short book distilling the points you consider most enduring—and worth continued pondering—from your writing about America's highest political and governmental office?

His query-cum-proposal is this book. In drafting each chapter, I looked back to see whether there might be what you could call "a useable past" from earlier compositions—veins of analysis to revisit and quarry again for these pages. Emerson considered "a foolish consistency" to be "the hobgoblin of little minds." For better or for worse, most of my thinking about presidential matters hasn't fluctuated very much over the years. For instance, I have written a dozen or so essays about the deficiency, unfairness, and—to be perfectly clear, as Richard Nixon was wont to say—idiocy of the current presidential-nominating system, which began in the 1970s and has gotten decidedly more ridiculous since then. This book's fifth chapter takes up the topic yet again, and I'll go to my grave speaking out in favor of reform—unless a more sensible system comes into being. I'm not holding my breath.

I'm most grateful to Steve Wrinn and to his efficient and cheerful colleagues at Notre Dame Press for their work on this book, the fifth one the press has published dealing (in one way or another) with White House campaigning and governing. In particular, the following people kindly helped at different stages of the process: Eli Bortz, editor in chief; Matthew Dowd, managing editor; Ann Donahue, copy editor; Wendy McMillen, production and design manager, and Kathryn Pitts, marketing manager. Sincere thanks to each of them.

This book is dedicated to William Hudson Giles, a friend of over a half century and the patron of the long-established Giles Fund at the University of Notre Dame that is now helping to support and enhance the work of Notre Dame Press. Bill's generosity to his alma mater—from which he graduated in 1967—is both providential and protean. To call him a loyal son of Notre Dame borders on understatement.

If I began to thank every editor of a publication or director of a lecture series responsible for the assignments leading to this book, authorial appreciation would resemble in length an entire chapter. Suffice it to say, I am deeply indebted to many women and men for working with me on the composition and delivery of earlier efforts, written and spoken, about the presidency.

I am also deeply grateful to the faculty, staff, and students of the Department of American Studies at the University of Notre Dame, where I taught from 1980 until arriving at emeritus status in 2018. For nearly forty years, classroom sessions served as the testing, if not proving, grounds for much of the analysis set down in these pages. Student questions and comments sharpened more than a few of those efforts at interpretation.

Tom Bettag, a faculty member at the University of Maryland's Merrill School of Journalism and executive producer of network news programs at CBS, ABC, NBC, and CNN for several decades, and Robert Costa, a national political reporter at the *Washington Post* and the moderator of *Washington Week* on PBS, read the book in manuscript form and offered incisive suggestions for improvement. Bountiful thanks to both of them.

Judy Schmuhl creates such an ideal domestic environment for writing that I don't plan to stop scribbling for the foreseeable future. But I promise to help with household chores now that I can no longer plead (or prevaricate) that I need time to prepare a class session or grade a stack of written assignments. She deserves that pledge—and much, much more. Mike Schmuhl knows the contemporary political landscape better than his old man and kindly read sections of this book as they were coming into being.

Any errors, however, are traceable to the author, who didn't know any better. He hereby formally apologizes for those mistakes, wherever they might be, and also for repeating certain points or facts in different places throughout this book. The repetition seemed necessary to clarify the consideration of a particular argument in the context of the explanation where it appears in one chapter or another. During the 1940 presidential campaign, supporters of the Republican candidate, Wendell Willkie, sported buttons opposing Franklin Roosevelt's third term that (somewhat suggestively) proclaimed: "NO MAN IS GOOD THREE TIMES." Occasionally, an author thinks that driving home a point two or even three times emphasizes that point's significance for a reader. Let's hope that makes sense to you.

INDEX

Bush, George W. (*cont.*)
  popular vote lost by, 93
  staff, size of, 30
  term limits and, 87, 91
Bush, Jeb, 70
BuzzFeed, 65

Camp David Accords, 150
campaign spending, 66
Capen, Nahum, xvi
Caro, Robert, *The Years of Lyndon Johnson*, 140–41
Carter, Jimmy
  change, voter proclivity for, 2, 5, 7–8, 10, 11
  in chronology of American presidency, 150–51
  Ford and, 97
  generational trends in presidency and, 19, 20, 24
  news conferences under, 98
  nominating/elections process and, 83
  as outsider candidate, xiv, 8
  Reagan versus, 106
  Southern states voting for, 40
CBS, 45, 61, 69, 103, 105, 106, 118, 119, 120, 131, 135, 167
Center for Responsive Politics, 105
change, voter proclivity for, 1–17
  candidate-centered nomination/election process affecting, 5–7, 11, 14–16
  first-time aspirants preference for, 5, 10–11
  increasing volatility of, 1–3
  outsider status, voter preference for, 7–10
  personality differences, voters favoring, 10
  regular cycle of elections influencing, 11–13
  term limits affecting, 3–5, 11–14
  trust in federal government, loss of, 9

"Checkers" speech, 145
Chester, Robert J., xvi
Chicago Democratic national convention (1968), 5–6, 78, 148
Chicago Tribune, xii–xiii
China, Nixon in, 148
Christian Science Monitor, xiii–xiv
Chua, Amy, *Political Tribes* (2018), 116
Civil Rights Act (1957), 145
Civil Rights Act (1964), 39–40, 141, 147
civil rights movement, 39–40, 78, 145, 147
Civil War, 21, 29, 37
Clapper, James, 125
Clay, Henry, 25
Cleveland, Grover, 21, 28, 93
Clinton, Bill
  George H. W. Bush and, 97
  change, voter proclivity for, 2, 5, 8, 10, 11, 13–14
  in chronology of American presidency, 153–55
  generational trends in presidency and, 20, 24–27, 35
  impeachment of, 27, 35, 44–46
  media and, 60, 64
  midterm elections under, 13, 43, 44, 154
  news conferences under, 98
  partisanship and polarization, increase in, 44–46, 56
  running for second term, 87, 88, 91
  Trump compared, 124–25, 126
  views on presidency, 29
Clinton, Hillary R.
  in 2016 election, 84, 93, 102, 103, 105, 106, 108, 156, 158
  change, voter proclivity for, 8, 15, 16
  media and, 52, 70
  popular but not Electoral College vote won by, 93

Republican Party (*cont.*)
  personal views of Democrats,
    54–55
  Southern/Southwestern switch
    to, 39–40
  Trump and, 104, 107, 115
  trust levels of voters and, 9
  weakening of major parties as
    political institutions, 15, 16
  See also change, voter proclivity
    for; nominating/election
    process; partisanship and
    polarization
Revolutionary War, 37
Romney, Mitt, 26, 80–81, 157
Roosevelt, Franklin Delano (FDR)
  change, voter proclivity for, 1, 4,
    14
  in chronology of American presi-
    dency, 144
  Cleveland and, 28
  "Fireside Chats," 116
  generational trends in presidency
    and, 19, 20, 32–33, 37
  ill health of, 89
  midterm elections under, 86
  New Deal programs continued
    by Eisenhower, 56
  news conferences under, 98
  Nixon compared, 22
  popular vote won in all elections
    by, 93
  State of the Union address under,
    98
  Supreme Court, efforts to pack,
    32
  term limits and presidency of,
    32–33, 85–86, 167
  Trump compared, xv, 109,
    116
Roosevelt, Theodore (TR)
  generational trends in presidency
    and, 1, 21, 30, 32, 37
  media and, 62
  term limits and, 85, 92

"White House" as name for
  presidential mansion and,
  xvi–xvii
Rossiter, Clinton, *The American
  Presidency*, 33
Rubio, Marco, 70
Russert, Tim, 74
Russia investigation, 121–22, 158,
  159
Ryan, Paul, 115, 135

Sadat, Anwar, 150
Safire, William, *Safire's Political
  Dictionary*, 49
Sanders, Bernie, 15, 104
Santorum, Rick, 80
Scalia, Antonin, 12
Schieffer, Bob, 131
Schlesinger, Arthur M., Jr.
  The Imperial Presidency, 34
  *War and the American Presi-
    dency*, 35
Schumer, Chuck, 48, 132
"second-term slump," 87–89
separation and balance of powers,
  78–79
September 11, 2001, 27, 35, 155
Sessions, Jeff, 129
sexual scandals, 27, 44, 45, 126,
  154–55
60 Minutes (TV show), 110, 120
slavery, presidency compared to,
  28
Smithsonian National Museum of
  American History, Wash-
  ington, D.C., xvi
social media. *See* media; *specific
  outlets, e.g.* Twitter
Soros, George, 52
Southern/Southwestern switch
  from Democrat to Republican,
  39–40
Spygate, 127–28
staff, presidential, 29–30
Stahl, Leslie, 120

Robert Schmuhl is the Walter H. Annenberg-Edmund P. Joyce Chair Emeritus in American Studies and Journalism, University of Notre Dame. He is the author of eight previous books with the University of Notre Dame Press, including *Fifty Years with Father Hesburgh: On and Off the Record* (2016, 2018).